At Issue

Are Executives Paid Too Much?

Other Books in the At Issue Series:

At Issue

Are Executives Paid Too Much?

Beth Rosenthal, Book Editor

GREENHAVEN PRESS
A part of Gale, Cengage Learning

GALE
CENGAGE Learning·

Detroit • New York • San Francisco • New Haven, Conn • Waterville, Maine • London

Elizabeth Des Chenes, *Managing Editor*

© 2012 Greenhaven Press, a part of Gale, Cengage Learning

Gale and Greenhaven Press are registered trademarks used herein under license.

For more information, contact:
Greenhaven Press
27500 Drake Rd.
Farmington Hills, MI 48331-3535
Or you can visit our Internet site at gale.cengage.com

Articles in Greenhaven Press anthologies are often edited for length to meet page requirements. In addition, original titles of these works are changed to clearly present the main thesis and to explicitly indicate the author's opinion. Every effort is made to ensure that Greenhaven Press accurately reflects the original intent of the authors. Every effort has been made to trace the owners of copyrighted material.

Cover image copyright © Images.com/Corbis.

LIBRARY OF CONGRESS CATALOGING-IN-PUBLICATION DATA

Are executives paid too much? / Beth Rosenthal, book editor.
    p. cm. -- (At issue)
  Includes bibliographical references and index.
  ISBN 978-0-7377-5888-7 (hardcover) -- ISBN 978-0-7377-5889-4 (pbk.)
  1. Executives--Salaries, etc. 2. Bonus system. I. Rosenthal, Beth, 1964-
  HD38.2.A74 2012
  658.4'072--dc23
                                                      2011037691

Printed in the United States of America
  1 2 3 4 5   15 14 13 12 11
FD342

Contents

Introduction

There are many opinions about where to place the blame for the financial crisis that began in 2007, including greedy Wall Street executives, American homeowners who depended too heavily on credit, and the government for not anticipating the crisis and dealing with it effectively. Whether Wall Street executives are to blame or not, many people were—and continue to be—outraged by the salaries and compensation packages that many executives receive.

The American Federation of Labor and Congress of Industrialized Organizations (AFL-CIO) website, www.paywatch.org, reports that CEOs were paid more than 343 times the salary of an average American worker, earning an average of $11.4 million in 2010. The gap between the wealthiest and poorest Americans continues to grow. Writing for the Associated Press on September 28, 2010, Hope Yen reports that US Census data show that "The top-earning 20 percent of Americans—those making more than $100,000 each year—received 49.4 percent of all income generated in the United States, compared with the 3.4 percent made by the bottom 20 percent of earners, those who fell below the poverty line. That ratio of 14.5-to-1 was an increase from 13.6 in 2008 and nearly double a low of 7.69 in 1968. At the top, the wealthiest 5 percent of Americans, who earn more than $180,000, added slightly to their annual incomes last year, the data show. Families at the $50,000 median level slipped lower."

While some feel that income inequality is inherently unfair and traps lower-income individuals into lifestyles from which they cannot escape, others question why income inequality has to be considered a problem at all. David Weinberger, writing for the Heritage Foundation on March 11, 2011, states that today most Americans can buy televisions and cars and take vacations, expenses that had been affordable only to the wealthy in the past. "All of this is available to us and our lives are made better off precisely because of the rich. Somebody got rich designing the iPhone. Somebody else got rich developing the laptop. And still someone else had to get rich building a more efficient vehicle. In other words, how is it possible, assuming one operates within the confines of the law, that somebody becomes rich without inevitably improving the standard of living for others? So, rather than begrudging the rich, we should be thankful that we benefit from their prosperity."

Others note that the jobs available are skewing more and more to one extreme or the other in terms of the skills needed and salaries offered. "At one end of job growth, you have increasing numbers of people flipping burgers, answering telephones, engaged in child care, mopping hallways, and in other low-wage lines of work. At the other end, you have increasing numbers of engineers, doctors, lawyers, and people in high-wage 'creative' careers. What's disappearing is the middle, the decent-paying jobs that helped expand the American middle class in the mid-twentieth century and that, if the present lopsided recovery is any indication, are now going the way of typewriters and landline telephones," writes Andy Kroll in "How the McEconomy Bombed the American Worker," on May 8, 2011, for tomdispatch.com.

Economists agree that this disparity has been growing for the last generation or so, but not everyone agrees about what—if anything—should be done about it. On the website inequality.org on June 2, 2011, Chuck Collins urges the government to make spending cuts and end tax cuts to the wealthy. "Spending cuts should start with our bloated Pentagon budget. We can save trillions by eliminating obsolete weapons systems and closing a third of US military bases around the world that add little to our security. Cut corporate welfare to agribusiness and oil companies, and we can raise another $ 1 trillion over the next decade. On the revenue side, lawmakers should reverse the half-century of tax cuts to millionaires and global corporations. If we taxed millionaires and corporations under the same rules we had in place in 1961, we'd generate $716 billion a year."

However, the role that government should play is up for debate as well. Former General Electric CEO and author Jack Welch and business journalist and commentator Suzy Welch write in the July 14, 2008, issue of *BusinessWeek*: "Government involvement? Forget it! What a mess that would be, with grandstanding politicians vying to outdo each other with vows of putting chief executives in the poorhouse and CEOs (and their lawyers) appearing at Capitol Hill hearings every year to explain their business models, describe their competitive situations, and defend pay packages as they relate to both. Now there's a productive use of everyone's time!"

The issue of executive salaries and compensation is just one aspect of the raging debate about solutions to help resolve the US financial crisis. In *At Issue: Are Executives Paid Too Much?*, the authors discuss the complexities involved in trying to determine just how much anyone should be paid for a job. The topics debated in this volume include whether or not shareholders' authority over executives' salaries should be increased, the role that salary plays in attracting the best people for a job, whether high salaries should be capped, the role that government should play in regulating salaries and compensation, the effect of executive salaries on the economy, and whether executive compensation should be tied to a company's profitability.

1

Compensation Committees Should Use Reason to Limit Executives' Salaries

Mark W. Olson

Mark W. Olson is the co-chair of Treliant Risk Advisors LL. He has served as a Federal Research governor, chair of the Public Company Accounting Oversight Board, and chairman of the American Bankers Association.

Determining executive pay can be difficult, but a common-sense approach often works best. Tying compensation to performance goals works well when there is a clear connection between an individual's job and financial revenue (such as someone who works on commission and who earns a portion of each transaction). Performance goals also work when compensation is tied to the performance of the company; the executive prospers when stock appreciates. However, problems occur when large compensation packages are earned by people working for less-than-successful companies. Compensation boards need to keep in mind that the compensation policy must be well communicated and seen as being fair; common sense needs to be used; and caps should be set up so that less-than-successful companies do not have employees earning more than seems justified.

One of the endearing memories of Olson family holiday lore is the time our (then) 3-year-old nephew John looked over the dinner table at a prepared feast and announced, "I want too much."

His blunt admission represented a combination of the hearty appetite of an active little boy and an affirmation that at age 3 he wanted to be shed of portion restraints imposed on him by adults. His statement generated a good laugh by the adults, but to John's chagrin, the portion restraints remained.

"I want too much" aptly described the appetite of many on Wall Street during the high-flying environment of the past decade; it resulted in, among other things, new regulations by banking regulators, legislative initiatives in the Dodd-Frank [Wall Street Reform and Consumer Protection] Act and general scorn by Wall Street observers.

How Much Compensation Is Too Much?

But despite the regulations, legislation and loud condemnation, a real question facing the financial services profession and indeed all of corporate America has emerged: How much is too much? The question is complicated because the definition of compensation has changed over the years, making comparisons difficult.

For example, the highest marginal income tax rate was 91% through World War II and continuing until 1964.

How much is too much? The question is complicated because the definition of compensation has changed over the years, making comparisons difficult.

During those years of literally confiscatory tax rates, it would have been lunacy for corporations to pay salaries in excess of $200,000 when the government would get all but 9% of those highest-taxed incomes. Few corporate execs in those days received even six-figure salaries; a $100,000-per-year salary was taxed at 70% on the marginal dollar.

But this doesn't mean that executives in those days were not well compensated. Corporations found many ways to provide perks that were both untaxed for the recipient and deductible for the corporation. The perks also went largely unreported in corporate financial documents, as there was no requirement to report them.

The 1980s and 1990s brought changes. The top marginal tax rates were gradually lowered, until the top marginal rate in 1990 was 28%.

Not surprisingly, taxable cash compensation at publicly traded companies soared, and so did the howls of protest when some of those wages seemed out of line with corporate performance. In 1993, that dissatisfaction resulted in legislation that denied a deduction on any compensation above $1 million unless the amount was determined "solely on account of the attainment of one or more performance goals."

Using Performance Goals to Avoid Restrictive Laws

How did corporate America respond to that new environment? Hello performance goals.

Performance goals work best in one of two circumstances. First, they work well when there is a tight correlation between individual initiative and a financial transaction. Thus, commission salespeople like stockbrokers and real estate agents who earn a portion on each transaction can readily justify performance goals. Their compensation arrangements go largely unchallenged as a matter of public policy because the correlation is well understood and accepted.

Even Lady Gaga's $65 million in earnings for 2009 drew less attention than her attire at a recent awards ceremony, because the link between her music sales and income is easily understood.

The second circumstance when such goals work is when compensation is aligned with corporate performance over time. The most obvious examples include instances in which founders of companies become billionaires due to the appreciation of their stock. Bill Gates and Richard Branson are rarely faulted for becoming extravagantly rich; their reward for their efforts is understood and largely accepted. Applying that concept in most managerial circumstances is more problematic.

Bill Gates and Richard Branson are rarely faulted for becoming extravagantly rich; their reward for their efforts is understood and largely accepted. Applying that concept in most managerial circumstances is more problematic.

Corporate Compensation Can Improve Shareholder Value

But since the mid-1990s, when the investor community began pushing the concept of "shareholder value," investors have been willing to appropriately compensate corporate leadership that enhances shareholder value over a defined period.

So, if these two concepts are generally acknowledged and are applicable in most organizations, why is compensation management so difficult? There are several reasons.

First, tax rates have greatly influenced compensation strategies over the years and comparisons of current compensation in a 35% top rate compared to a 91% top rate are not valid unless adjusted for the tax and perk differences.

Second, the link is complicated when high-performing employees work for underperforming companies. Thus, certain traders on Wall Street who had achieved astonishingly high performance targets were widely vilified if they had the misfortune of being employed by companies receiving taxpayer bailouts.

Of course, the press attention received in the most egregious of these instances has had a chilling impact on everybody else.

So, what guidelines should compensation committees follow when making policy decisions?

Use Common Sense to Determine Appropriate Compensation

First, remember that even at the highest levels, compensation has the potential to be a negative motivator. There is no better evidence of this than the whines and complaints of highly paid professional athletes. The same dissatisfaction can exist in any organization if the compensation philosophy is not well communicated and not perceived to be fair.

Second, adopt a common-sense rule that is grounded by industry norms. Even when compensation within an organization is perceived to be fair and well understood, an organization needs to compare its approach with industry norms. There are plenty of experts willing to help an organization justify ever-higher salaries, but the common-sense test should help establish parameters that keep an organization from awarding compensation at levels that are perceived as unjustified.

Third, when evaluating compensation for commission salespeople, companies need to establish caps in order to avoid circumstances in which underperforming companies have the industry's highest-paid people or when a single individual in an organization earns many times what others at a similar level earn.

Compensation committees at corporations will continue to be a focus of attention over the next few years. The above approaches are tools that can help them manage that responsibility.

2

Executives Must Be Paid Well in Order to Attract Top Talent

Dominic Basulto

Dominic Basulto is the editor of Fortune Business Innovation Insider.

Many Americans believe the myth that Chief Executive Officers (CEOs) are overpaid. Arguments that the average CEO makes more than 300 times than the average American worker need to be put in the proper perspective. The average corporate CEO earns less than those who work at hedge funds, private equity firms, and investment banks. This should be of concern to all because it could mean that many qualified people will turn to money management positions, which pay better. The belief that CEOs control the compensation boards is not true because recent legislation has closed such loopholes and has increased the power of the board of directors. Increasingly, too, CEOs are fired when they cannot generate satisfactory results. People with general management skills now are being hired for positions, sometimes from entirely different industries, rather than those with experience in a particular field. Those who might have been CEOs are going to firms that pay more, have less control from a board of directors, and less attention from the public.

A recent Gallup poll found that only one in six Americans thinks highly of business executives. Is it any wonder? This past year—in addition to the unceremonious exits of

Dominic Basulto, "Why Do We Underpay Our Best CEOs?" *The American*, December 5, 2006. Copyright © 2006 by The American Enterprise Institute. Reproduced with permission of *The American* Magazine, a national magazine of politics, business, and culture (www.american.com).

chief executives from such companies as Bristol-Myers Squibb and Viacom, and the convictions of two Enron CEOs—there was the scandal over backdating stock-option grants and the revelations at Hewlett-Packard of prying into telephone records. Meanwhile, the average CEO of a large, publicly traded American company now has annual compensation of $10.5 million—or about 300 times higher than the average U.S. worker. "How do I feel about executive compensation?" said John Bogle, founder of Vanguard mutual funds. "Terrible." CEO pay packages are "outrageous" and "inexcusable," he added.

The Best and Brightest Will Go Where There's More Money

But are they really? In fact, there's strong evidence that, far from being paid too much, many CEOs are paid too little. Not only do the top managers of multibillion-dollar corporations earn less than basketball players (LeBron James of the Cleveland Cavaliers makes $26 million), they are also outpaced in compensation by financial impresarios at hedge funds, private equity firms, and investment banks. Should we care? Yes. If other positions pay far more, then the best and the brightest minds will be drawn away from running major businesses to pursuits that may not be as socially useful—if not to the basketball court, then to money management.

Still, the legend of the overpaid CEO persists. A widely accepted explanation for excessive CEO pay goes like this: Contrary to the theory that a board of directors sets the boss's pay in order to maximize profits for shareholders, powerful CEOs actually control boards. Directors owe their well-paying positions to the chief executive, so they give him a pay package far in excess of what it should be. The compensation committee of the board of directors effectively acts as a rubber stamp for the CEO. How else, we are told, can we explain the fantastically high pay packages of the likes of Richard Grasso and Dennis Kozlowski?

Three law school professors—Lucian Bebchuk of Harvard, Jesse Fried of the University of California at Berkeley, and David Walker of Brown—laid out this argument in an influential academic paper titled "Managerial Power and Rent Extraction in the Design of Executive Compensation." It's a simple story with obvious media appeal.

If other positions pay far more, then the best and the brightest minds will be drawn away from running major businesses to pursuits that may not be as socially useful. . . .

While the explanation is undoubtedly true in some cases, it is less than satisfactory as a general proposition, especially at a time when Sarbanes-Oxley legislation has closed the kind of managerial-power loopholes that might have been exploited by some CEOs, and has instead elevated the authority of directors. And, in an age when shareholders judge performance on a quarterly basis, the CEO who fails to produce results is often shown the door by directors rather than dominating them. According to executive recruiter Challenger, Gray & Christmas, in the first half of this year, 728 chief executive officers lost their jobs. That number was 6.9 percent higher than the same period last year, which itself set a record.

If Bebchuk and his colleagues are mistaken, then what is the theoretical model that offers a convincing market-based explanation for the hiring trends in the CEO marketplace? Two professors at the University of Southern California's Marshall School of Business, Kevin J. Murphy and Jan Zabojnik, may have the answer. They start with the observation that big businesses in recent years have been hiring more outsiders— that is, CEOs who don't work for the company that is bringing them on, or even in the same industry. In addition, the outsiders make more money than the insiders. (You would expect that, if anything, directors would be more beholden to insiders.)

More Hiring from the Outside

These two developments, according to Murphy and Zabojnik, reflect a fundamental change in the types of managerial skills required to run large companies. General managerial skills like finance, marketing, and strategy are increasingly more important than firm-specific skills, such as understanding the drug pipeline of a pharmaceutical company or knowing how to negotiate with a steel company's suppliers, unions, and big customers. In the 1970s, outside hires accounted for 15 percent of all new CEOs; in the 1980s, there was a small increase to 17 percent; and in the 1990s, a larger jump to 27 percent.

In the past, a firm typically promoted from within, preferring to select someone with a proven track record within a certain industry. At times, companies might have hired a former McKinsey consultant with broader experience, or poached a star manager from an unofficial CEO training ground like General Electric. More commonly, an automaker, for example, would hire a CEO from the auto industry, a consumer-electronic manufacturer from consumer electronics.

But that is changing. IBM made one of the best CEO hires in history when it went far afield in 1993 to select Lou Gerstner, who had been chief executive of RJR Nabisco for four years and had spent 11 years at American Express before that. On September 5, 2006, Ford Motor Company hired as its CEO Alan Mulally, who came straight from Boeing, where he had worked since 1969.

As markets grow increasingly globalized and information—thanks to the Internet—becomes more accessible, it's not hard to see why boards of directors are going outside their companies and industries to find CEOs. But, if aviation and packaged-goods executives are added to the pool of CEO candidates for an auto company, doesn't that increase supply and thus drive down price? Shouldn't compensation fall rather than rise?

Not necessarily. The variety of candidates in the pool may increase, but not the number. In the past, companies were content to promote from within because they did not need someone with, for example, broad strategic and financial experience in the greater world. Now, they do, but such folks aren't easy to find. In fact, it's likely that the supply of top-notch CEOs for global companies is leveling off or even falling.

Losing Potential CEOs to Privately Held Companies

One reason for this is that the smartest potential CEOs are being siphoned off by higher-paid professions where public scrutiny and board control are less pronounced. After all, the same talent pool that produces doctors, lawyers, portfolio managers, and investment bankers also produces a fair share of CEOs. When it comes to compensation, the peer group for a CEO is not just the CEO next door, but also the venture capitalist on the other side of the country, or the investment banker on the other side of the world.

The latest statistics from Holt Private Equity Consultants and Dow Jones Private Equity Analyst show that the average employee at a venture capital firm will receive $770,000 in total compensation this year while the average employee of a private-equity firm earns $1.2 million. That's the average employee, not the boss. Senior partners at venture firms earn about $1.5 million, general partners $2 million. Even those figures pale in comparison to hedge funds. According to *Institutional Investor* magazine, average compensation for the top 25 hedge fund managers was $251 million in 2004—that's more than 20 times as much as the average CEO. Leading the pack was Edward Lampert, who earned just over $1 billion.

Charles Munger, who is Warren Buffett's close associate at Berkshire Hathaway, Inc., and heads Wesco Financial himself, has eloquently lamented these developments. "I regard the amount of brainpower going into money management as a national scandal," he said at Wesco's annual meeting. "I think it's crazy to have incentives that drive your most intelligent people into a very sophisticated gaming system." The incentive, of course, is money. There may be not enough of it in running public companies, and too much of it elsewhere.

Private equity, or buyout, firms—which use cash from investors such as pension funds to purchase companies, refurbish, and then sell them—now have $1 trillion in assets. When they enter the market for CEO talent, they aren't shy about offering high pay and demanding high performance. David Calhoun, a former vice chairman of GE, was recently picked by a group of buyout firms to lead a privately held Dutch company called VNU, which owns *Billboard* and *The Hollywood Reporter*, among other properties. Press reports valued his total compensation package at $100 million. Clearly, Calhoun wasn't extracting excess rents from a captive board. He was paid well because private firms have more room to offer market prices to CEOs than public ones. Wrote Geoffrey Colvin in *Fortune*: "Any public company that now offered a new CEO $100 million would be scourged without mercy by shareholder activists and TV talking heads nationwide."

It's Difficult to Anticipate CEO Performance

A CEO should be paid according to what he is expected to produce. But how to anticipate his performance? If Alex Rodriguez hit 40 or more homers and drove in 130 or more runs as a Texas Ranger, was it wrong for New York fans to assume that he would do the same as a New York Yankee? Likewise, if a super-star CEO delivered 10 percent year-over-year earnings growth and a 50 percent increase in the share price during a tenure elsewhere, is it wrong to assume that he will do the same at his next destination?

Unfortunately, there is little way of knowing whether the past is prologue—and, as it turns out, little correlation between CEO pay and stock performance—as detractors delight in pointing out. In fact, the market for CEOs is not much different from the market for money managers, most of whom—educated at the best schools in the nation and paid extremely well—fail to beat the Standard & Poor's 500 Stock Index. And it is extremely difficult to predict whether managers who beat the index this year will do so next year.

A CEO should be paid according to what he is expected to produce. But how to anticipate his performance?

Those few portfolio managers who do manage to beat the S&P 500 benchmark fairly consistently (think Buffett) are said to possess "positive alpha"—that is, their actual returns are better than expected returns when you consider the amount of risk they assume. If the primary role of the CEO is to allocate capital efficiently and maximize the profitability (and thus, the stock price) of the firm, then the duty of a board of directors is to identify CEO candidates with positive alpha. Steve Jobs of Apple seems to have it, as did Jack Welch at GE and Lou Gerstner at IBM. In an efficient market, one would expect that only a small percentage of CEOs would be able to beat expectations and turn in superior performance.

One way to match pay with performance is to offer incentive pay, but, even with such a package, a CEO presents a risky bet for a board since, if he underperforms for two years, the savings in pay don't come close to the loss in expected profits or decline in stock price. And, even with incentives that link pay to stock prices or profits, the mismatch between compensation and performance can be extreme—down as well as up. Some CEOs are clearly underpaid. *Forbes* recently calculated that, over the past six years, Robert K. Cole, CEO of New Century Financial—a company with a market capitalization of $2.2 billion—received average annual compensation of only $1.6 million while his company's stock returned 36 percent yearly. Over the same period, Mark Pigott, CEO of Paccar, made just $3.1 million annually while his company's stock returned 30 percent a year.

A CEO's Compensation Can Be Dwarfed by Soaring Profits

Let's go back to Alan Mulally. He is reportedly being paid more than $15 million in annual compensation to turn around the ailing carmaker, and, if he meets his performance targets over the next two years, his compensation could reach as high as $34 million. Is that too low or too high? As a Ford spokesperson explains, the level of compensation is simply the market rate, and that is the only rate that matters: "Mr. Mulally's compensation was based on the competitive environment for world-class talent, the demands of the position, and the need to recruit Mr. Mulally from a long, established career at Boeing." Ultimately, the answer to the question of whether Mulally is underpaid or overpaid rests on whether he will find the right deployment of capital to satisfy Wall Street investors, and in doing so, lift the company's stock price. If he can, then he is worth every penny of that salary—and a lot more.

In early October, Ford's market capitalization was $15 billion. If Ford can be restored to profitability in the next two or three years, it's not difficult to imagine a market cap of $25 billion or more. If Mulally is paid $50 million or even $100 million to pull off such a huge gain, would the compensation be worthwhile? Of course. Even at $100 million, the leverage is spectacular.

An able leader has an enormous impact on the success of a business. Certainly, some excessive corporate pay packages are "outrageous," as Bogle and other critics claim. But even more outrageous is a system where Dr. Phil makes more than twice as much as Jeffrey Immelt, CEO of GE, the world's most valuable company; where Jessica Simpson makes more than the average earned by the CEOs of America's 500 largest corporations; and where hedge fund managers who make the right bet on the yen-dollar relationship can take home ten times as much as the head of the nation's largest exporter.

[E]ven more outrageous is a system where Dr. Phil makes more than twice as much as Jeffrey Immelt, CEO of GE, the world's most valuable company. . . .

Because of the growing complexity of the corporate leadership role and the paucity of CEOs with positive alpha, it's almost certain that pay will rise—at least among companies that are not listed on stock exchanges and subject to the regulatory regime of Sarbanes-Oxley and media scrutiny of compensation. CEO pay at some of the largest and most important publicly traded companies, however, may remain constrained. That's not a good thing—not for those businesses, their shareholders, or the economy as a whole.

3

CEOs Want to Hide the Gap Between Worker Pay and Their Own

Sam Pizzigati

Sam Pizzigati, an associate editor at the Institute for Policy Studies, also writes an online weekly column called "Too Much."

The Dodd-Frank executive pay legislation includes a "say on pay" provision, in which shareholders are assured a chance to place "advisory" votes on the salary packages for CEOs. Corporate boards do not want to give shareholders any real control over executive pay, but feel they will be able to adjust how pay packages are put together enough to continue doing business as usual. However, they will balk at Sen. Bob Menendez' (D-NJ) directive that requires corporations to annually divulge the specific gap between their CEO's salary and the average salary of their employees. This would put corporations in the position of having to explain why their CEO is so much more worthy of earning a higher salary. The Securities and Exchange Commission is being pressured to water down Menendez's provision, including allowing corporations to count only the salaries of full-time American workers. Proponents of the mandate argue that, because many Americans are invested in these companies through pension funds, employee salaries should be released.

Sam Pizzigati, "The Paycheck Data CEOs Don't Want Us to See," OurFuture.org, January 9, 2011. Copyright © 2011 by Institute for America's Future. Reproduced by permission.

Sometimes lobbyists—even the most perfectly coiffed—mess up. Lobbyists for Corporate America messed up big-time last summer. They let slip into law, via the 2,300-page Dodd-Frank financial reform bill, an obscure provision that could give future lawmakers a powerful lever for ratcheting down excessive CEO pay.

Now those lobbyists are pushing hard to undo their mistake—and progressives, led by AFL-CIO [American Federation of Labor and Congress of Industrialized Organizations] president Rich Trumka, are pushing back.

The winner won't be clear until later this year [2011] when the Securities and Exchange Commission [SEC], the federal watchdog agency over Wall Street, releases the final regulations that will enforce the Dodd-Frank legislation.

That legislation includes an assortment of provisions that impact executive pay. One of these—"say on pay"—has been receiving a good bit of media attention. This "say on pay" guarantees shareholders a regular opportunity to cast "advisory" votes on the CEO pay packages that corporate boards produce.

Corporations Want to Continue Doing Business as Usual

Corporate boards don't particularly like the idea of letting shareholders vote on CEO pay, but most have come around to understanding that, by just tweaking how they structure their CEO pay packages, they can continue conducting CEO pay business as usual even with "say on pay" on the books.

Indeed, several other nations—including Britain—already give shareholders the right to take advisory votes on executive pay. Executive pay, in these nations, has kept right on rising.

Corporate boards, in other words, can live with "say on pay." But they seem to be choking an another Dodd-Frank executive pay provision that Senator Bob Menendez from New Jersey slipped into the legislation at the eleventh hour.

This Menendez mandate requires America's corporations to disclose, for the first time ever, the specific gap between what they pay their CEO, on an annual basis, and what they pay their most typical workers.

Current law requires corporations to report how much their top five executives are making. Under the Menendez mandate, corporations must now also report their overall wage "median" and the ratio between this median and their top pay.

Corporate boards don't particularly like the idea of letting shareholders vote on CEO pay, but most have come around to understanding that, by just tweaking how they structure their CEO pay packages, they can continue conducting CEO pay business as usual even with "say on pay" on the books.

Companies Must Report the Ratio Between CEO and Average Worker

That information—from a public relations standpoint—could be explosive. CEOs who make 1,000 times more than their most typical workers would have to explain what makes them so much more valuable than competing CEOs who make just 100 times their worker pay.

But the impact of the Menendez mandate could go far beyond public relations. Future lawmakers could, for instance, deny lucrative government contracts to companies that pay their top executives over 100 times what they pay their workers—or 25 times, the CEO-worker pay ratio back in the mid 20th century.

In Britain, advocates for more reasonable executive pay levels are now making just this sort of proposal. The prospect of similar pressure here in the United States has Corporate

America shuddering—and pressing the Securities and Exchange Commission to water down the Dodd-Frank Menendez mandate.

The SEC can't, of course, kill the mandate outright. Pay ratio disclosure, after all, now stands as the law of the land. But the agency still must translate that law into enforceable specifics, and this translating will require a series of rulings, on a variety of fronts, that could mute the Menendez mandate's ultimate impact.

Including only full-time U.S. workers would let American corporations that outsource jobs or—load up on part-timers—to style themselves as noble "high-wage" employers.

One example: Should corporations be required, under the mandate, to figure into their median worker pay calculations the wages that go to part-timers or workers outside the United States?

Corporate trade groups like the American Benefits Council—an outfit that represents the bulk of the *Fortune* 500—want only full-time U.S. workers to be included. For obvious reasons. Including only full-time U.S. workers would let American corporations that outsource jobs—or load up on part-timers—to style themselves as noble "high-wage" employers.

Corporate lobbyists are also attacking the new Dodd-Frank pay ratio mandate as a "highly costly and burdensome" new obligation on corporations. They're asking the SEC to let companies offer up a "single employee" as "representative" of what they pay their workers, instead of requiring corporations to calculate what their median workers actually get paid.

AFL-CIO president Rich Trumka, in an official response filed last month shortly before the holidays, dubbed these corporate charges clearly "overblown."

Requirements Do Not Make More Work for Corporations

Corporations, Trumka pointed out, already have to file W-2 forms that report every American worker's total compensation. Foreign nations "have similar reporting requirements." And firms, he added, can easily prorate their part-time worker pay "to provide a more complete picture of workforce compensation."

The actual language of the Dodd-Frank law, the AFL-CIO leader went on to note, requires publicly traded companies to disclose "the median of the annual total compensation of all employees of the issuer,'" not just U.S. employees. Corporations could meet this requirement, Trumka suggests, simply by reporting the median pay of their U.S. and foreign workers "as two separate statistics."

"The retirement savings of America's working families ... depend in part on public companies having responsible compensation practices for both their CEOs and all other employees."

In any case, Trumka emphasizes, investors—and the public at large—need the information the Menendez mandate seeks to provide. A "meaningful disclosure of how employee compensation is allocated over their workforce" will help the public understand how corporations are approaching core operating issues.

Are these corporations, for instance, paying more than minimal wages to "attract the best qualified employees and improve employee productivity"?

Higher levels of median compensation, Trumka reminds the SEC in his statement, can "make it easier to retain workers and reduce employee turnover." And smaller disparities between the top and bottom of the corporate pay ladder, his

SEC comment adds, also strengthen enterprise "cohesion and teamwork," as the founder of modern management science, Peter Drucker, often argued.

Americans' Pensions Depend on Companies

Average Americans, Trumka's commentary makes clear, have still another reason to care deeply about Corporate America's pay practices. Everyday Americans have billions of pension dollars invested in U.S. corporations.

"The retirement savings of America's working families," says Trumka, "depend in part on public companies having responsible compensation practices for both their CEOs and all other employees."

Will the SEC agree—and come out with regulations that match the Menendez mandate's full-disclosure spirit? Or will the agency issue regs that let Corporate America off the hook? That answer remains months away.

In the meantime, a variety of public interest groups will be meeting this week in Washington, D.C., to kick off a new CEO pay taskforce—and help make sure SEC rulemakers hear from all America, not just the corporate lobbying set.

4

Executive Compensation Should Be Tied to Company Profitability

Clive Crook

Clive Crook is a contributing editor to the National Journal, *the chief Washington Affairs commentator for the* Financial Times, *and senior editor of the* Atlantic.

It is wrong for underperforming corporations to continue to pay huge compensation packages to their CEOs. Shareholders are "paying for failure" by continuing this practice. For example, Verizon is one of 11 large corporations that does just that; millions of dollars are paid out to executives, despite the millions that are lost in revenue. This is allowed to happen because compensation boards, in many cases, grant bonuses even if the corporation is underperforming. Another problem is that outside consultants, who may also work for the corporation, are sometimes hired by compensation boards, resulting in a conflict of interest. Shareholders need to exercise more control over compensation packages, and corporations should be required to disclose more information about compensation packages.

Nothing disgraces American capitalism so much as the enormous, and growing, disparity between the pay and performance of many top executives. With remorseless efficiency—and for the greater good of the country, as I usually try to argue—American free enterprise grinds away at almost every kind of cost, and notably the cost of labor. This process, brutal as it may seem, drives growth in productivity, in national income, and ultimately in living standards. It is the foundation, and the price, of America's economic success. That is what many a chief executive will tell you, as well, with all due gravity. But in so many cases, this zeal for control of costs is jarringly absent when it comes to those bosses' own pay. Many CEOs are gouging the owners of the companies they work for, and they are doing it shamelessly. Shareholders, unfortunately, keep letting them get away with it.

Every proxy season brings new evidence of amazing rapacity. In the past few days, *The Wall Street Journal, The New York Times, USA Today,* and other papers have run long and admirably detailed reports on the subject, drawing on the latest company filings. The theme of the coverage is not new by any means, nor are the particular instances in qualitative terms. In fact, people are getting inured to the issue, and that is only going to make things worse. Steadfast critics of capitalism express the usual outrage over these cases, of course, but that carries no weight: They are routinely outraged about so many things. It is the embarrassed silence of the defenders of capitalism that is so disappointing, and that really matters. Those people should be ashamed, and seen to be ashamed, of the injustice—of the brazen ethical failure—that lies behind each new crop of figures.

The New York Times, with good reason, paid particular attention to the case of Verizon. The firm's CEO, Ivan G. Seidenberg, received $19.4 million last year, in a mixture of salary, bonus, restricted stock, and other payments, a rise of nearly 50 percent over the previous year. That was justified, according to the company's compensation committee, because Seidenberg met some "challenging" performance benchmarks. So the company did well in 2005? Not exactly. Earnings fell by 5.5 percent, the company's shares dropped 26 percent, and its bonds were downgraded. The *Times* also reported that 50,000 of the firm's managers had their pensions frozen. (The company had a difficult year, you see: The pension freeze was doubtless a painful but necessary sacrifice.)

Verizon is on a list of 11 big companies accused of "paying for failure" by The Corporate Library, a corporate-governance research outfit. In a just-published study, TCL found that over the past five years board compensation committees "authorized a total of $865 million in pay to CEOs who presided over an aggregate loss of $640 billion in shareholder value." The 11 companies are AT&T, BellSouth, Hewlett-Packard, Home Depot, Lucent Technologies, Merck, Pfizer, Safeway, Time Warner, Verizon, and Wal-Mart. Each of these "paid their CEOs more than $15 million in the last two available fiscal years; had a negative return to stockholders over the last five years; and underperformed their peers over the same period."

But the problem goes much wider than this. Year in, year out, the median pay of top executives rises much faster than do overall wages and salaries. There is no reason why this should be so—not if the market for CEOs is working as rigorously as the market for other kinds of labor. But, of course, it is not. There is no economic rationale, no "incentivizing" justification, for enormous severance payments to departing (failed) CEOs, or for full-salary pensions worth eight figures or more, granted to bosses about to retire. The idea is a joke. The cases that TCL has drawn attention to, and the wider trend of rising CEO pay regardless of performance, show that the market for CEOs is broken.

That is a bad thing in itself—and, fairness aside, the scale of the resulting misallocation of resources is not small. An academic study published last year by Lucian Bebchuk and Yaniv Grinstein in the *Oxford Review of Economic Policy* estimated that from 2001 to 2003, the total pay of the five highest-earning CEOs of public companies was equivalent to nearly 10 percent of the companies' earnings, roughly double the share of earnings paid out that way from 1993 to 1995. Pay on that scale, if it elicits no improvement in company performance, is perceptibly depressing return on investment. That, as I say, is serious enough, but a far larger cost comes in damage to the system's reputation.

Year in, year out, the median pay of top executives rises much faster than do overall wages and salaries.

Most CEOs understand, or say they understand, that capitalism needs the tacit support of the public to function well. In fact, to judge by much popular culture, Americans are already fairly distrustful of capitalism—but these things are relative. If Americans were as hostile to big business as, say, the French are, then the tax and regulatory regime for American companies would quickly evolve to become as unfriendly and dysfunctional as France's. When compensation committees vote huge and patently unwarranted pay increases for their nonperforming CEOs, they are working to that end. They are not just failing in their duty to the shareholders whose interests they are paid to uphold, they are hurting the rest of us as well. They are undermining capitalism more surely than its avowed opponents and making its defenders look like spokesmen for base hypocrisy.

Can anything be done about it? For most corporate-governance activists, the remedy of first resort is greater disclosure. The Securities and Exchange Commission has a proposal that will oblige companies to give more information about the total pay of their top executives, making it easier to do a full accounting. This should go further.

In the face of opposition from business leaders, regulators are not pressing for disclosure of the performance formulas (if any) that compensation committees apply in designing CEOs' supposedly performance-related packages. That is a mistake. TCL's research points to cases where compensation committees authorize bonuses that start to pay out if the company stands at well below the median of the chosen measure of success. In other words, even if the company is doing worse than most of the firms in its segment, its CEO can expect to collect a bonus for good performance. Very challenging. Perhaps, if companies had to report schemes as ludicrous as this to shareholders and had to document them in detail, more compensation committees would hesitate to approve them.

The Times drew attention to another anomaly, reminiscent of the conflicts of interest that have plagued auditors and investment analysts. Many compensation committees use outside advisers to guide them and to sanctify the pay schemes they decide upon. But these advisers apparently do lots of other business—worth far more to them than the advice on CEO pay—with the firms concerned. They may design or manage the firm's employee-benefits system, for example. So they are giving advice on how much to pay the CEO at the same time that he or she is deciding how much other business to send their way. At the moment, companies do not have to disclose these relationships.

The answer lies in the combination of greater disclosure and greater power for shareholders.

But one may ask whether greater openness will be enough. Some businesses argue that disclosure will make matters worse—that easier comparisons of CEO pay will ramp up the money even more. It is an insincere argument, of course—"Please don't push my pay up even faster"—but it might actually be true, especially since many compensation committees appear to set pay, or elements of pay, at a percentile of CEO compensation across their industry. What an abject abdication of responsibility to shareholders that is. Moreover, if every CEO expects to be paid at least as well as the average, you

have a neverending upward spiral of cost—and fuller disclosure might then indeed make matters worse.

The answer lies in the combination of greater disclosure
and greater power for shareholders. We need both, so that the
owners can do something with the information. In short,
CEOs need to be made less secure. Regulatory and legal restraints on hostile takeovers—much the best discipline on
boards that forget their fiduciary responsibilities—need to be
rolled back. Also, public companies should be obliged to put
the fully disclosed pay of their top executives to an annual
shareholder vote (as in Britain), and (unlike in Britain) that
vote should be binding on the company.

Even then, shareholders would have to be willing to exert
themselves—something that, in America, they have often been
oddly reluctant to do. They lose a lot by their passivity, and
so, unfortunately, do the rest of us.

5

Executive Compensation Should Not Be Tied to Company Profitability

Robert P. Murphy

Robert P. Murphy is on the faculty at the Mises University, an adjunct scholar at the Mises Institute, is the author of The Politically Incorrect Guide to the Great Depression, *the* Study Guide to Man, Economy, and State with Power and Market, *and the* Human Action Study Guide, *and runs the blog* Free Advice.

It is unfair to claim that CEO compensation should be linked to the profitability of a corporation. In a competitive workplace, some employees are paid more because they bring additional profits to their boss. If the salary of an average worker (for example, an assembly-line worker at General Motors) is not affected when the stock of that company drops, it is not fair to expect that the Chief Executive Officer's salary should be. Additionally, the corporate world might lose some valuable executives if their contracts specify that the amount of their compensation will fluctuate depending on the company's profits. We should also assume that shareholders are careful with their money and realize that the executives are worth the large salaries they command.

One of *Reader's Digest*'s more popular sections is "That's Outrageous!" When the feature spotlights government pork-barrel projects, absurd zoning restrictions on homeown-

Robert P. Murphy, "Are CEOs Paid Too Much?" *Freeman*, vol. 56, October 2006. Copyright © 2006 by Foundation for Economic Education, Inc. Reproduced by permission.

ers, or illogical regulations on small business, libertarians can applaud. Unfortunately the October 2005 issue featured a column that focused on "outrageous" CEO packages, an enduring controversy. The writer, Michael Crowley, displayed precious little knowledge of economics, and at times his complaints were downright contradictory.

The article begins with the anecdote about Stephen Crawford, then the co-president of Morgan Stanley. A few months after accepting this promotion, Crawford quit during a "management shake-up" and "strolled off with a severance package that included two years' salary and bonus," which amounted to $32 million. To make sure his readers are sufficiently outraged, Crowley points out that "Crawford pulled in $54,000 per hour!"

Before delving into the conceptual issues, let's be clear on where that number comes from. It is obviously due to Crawford's quitting much sooner than anyone (probably including himself) predicted when the contract was originally negotiated. (Had the shakeup occurred six weeks earlier, Crawford would've earned over $100,000 per hour, according to this method.) This is certainly a misleading approach, especially when contrasting it with the mean annual earnings of workers (as Crowley does). If one wants to show how much more CEOs get paid—and of course they do get paid far, far more than the average worker—then a fairer comparison would have been mean annual earnings of workers versus mean annual earnings of CEOs. (Later, Crowley follows this more reasonable route and reports that in 2003 "CEOs were paid over 300 times what the average production worker made.") To pick an example like Crawford rigs the comparison; one could certainly find cases of average Joes who quit or were laid off after only working a very short time, and hence whose "hourly earnings" would appear vastly inflated.

For example, I myself was once sent home after only working about ten minutes as a receptionist in a law firm; I had been sent there by my temp agency, and it turned out I was unfamiliar with the phone system at the firm. Nonetheless, I still got paid for at least one hour (possibly more, I can't remember) of work. Using Crowley's approach, he could argue that the case of Robert Murphy shows that some Irish workers are paid six times more per hour than the median temp worker.

Even on its own terms, the calculation is suspect. Crowley isn't explicit about where the $54,000 per hour figure comes from, but we do know that the total package was $32 million and that Crawford quit "[a]bout 100 days" after starting in the new spot. Well, $32 million divided by 100 is $320,000 per day, which works out to $40,000 per hour if we assume eight hours of work per day. Thus to get the higher figure of $54,000, Crowley must be assuming that, in addition to working only eight hours per day, Crawford only worked five days per week. Now I don't know too much about being co-president of Morgan Stanley, but even so, I'm quite sure that this job requires more than 40 hours of work per week.

Some Jobs Are Worth More Than Other Jobs

Of course, these minor quibbles about the figure overlook the biggest objection: So what if CEOs earn more money than most other workers? In a free market (and below we deal with the complication that in today's world there is no truly free market), the price of labor corresponds to its marginal product. That is, competition ensures that workers are paid according to how much additional revenue they bring in to their employer. The fact that some types of labor command thousands of times more market value is no more surprising or outrageous than the fact that some goods in the marketplace (such as a house) have a price hundreds of thousands of times higher than the prices of other goods (such as a pack of gum).

Oddly enough, it is the critics of capitalism who implicitly claim that market value should correspond to ethical worth. No competent economist would argue that Stephen Crawford was a good person because he earned so much money, just as no economist would argue that a television set is ethically superior to a copy of the Holy Bible because of its higher price. No, the only thing economic science can say is that Stephen Crawford's services were in higher demand than the services of (say) the janitors at Morgan Stanley. So long as the labor contracts are voluntary, there really isn't an issue of fairness (subject to the complication noted above).

So what if CEOs earn more money than most other workers? In a free market . . . , the price of labor corresponds to its marginal product. That is, competition ensures that workers are paid according to how much additional revenue they bring in to their employer.

Later in the article, Crowley raises concerns that may trouble even a genuine supporter of the free market. Of course it makes perfect sense that successful corporate executives earn millions of dollars. But what of the strange cases of "corporate leaders actually failing their way to riches"? Crowley gives us some allegedly outrageous examples of this trend:

Viacom CEO Sumner Redstone took home about $28 million in 2004, including a bonus of $16.5 million, even as his company's stock dropped 11 percent during the fiscal year. Applied Materials CEO Mike Splinter got a tidy $5 million bonus in 2004, despite a stock slide of more than 22 percent. That same year Rick Wagoner, CEO of General Motors [GM], saw GM stock plunge 25 percent, yet he still pocketed a $2.5 million bonus—only slightly less than his award in 2003, when GM stock actually rose. So much for accountability.

As noted, this phenomenon is initially quite puzzling. Why would firms reward incompetent executives? Don't they want to make money? Yet before dismissing power brokers in the business community as self-destructive and/or incredibly stupid, perhaps we should give them the benefit of the doubt and search for a rational explanation.

Average Worker Salaries Are Not Affected by a Company's Stock

The most important point that scoffers like Crowley overlook is that the business world is uncertain. When a company brings in a new executive, it is not at all obvious what steps he or she should take to turn the company around and boost profits. (If it were obvious, the company wouldn't waste millions of dollars hiring the executive.) Now regardless of the executive's competence, it is entirely possible that the plan will fail—and the executive knows this as well as anyone else. Because of this, it would be very risky for such an executive to sign a contract in which, say, he or she earned $20 million if the company were profitable, but $50,000 if the company tanks. Rather than sign that contract, the executive (who must be quite skilled to be offered such a job in the first place) could consult or take a less glamorous position and earn, say, $5 million for sure.

This principle—that an executive gets paid handsomely even if the company does poorly—doesn't seem outrageous when the numbers are lower. For example, when GM stock plunged 25 percent, did Crowley expect the assembly-line workers to give back a quarter of their wages for that year? If not, why not? After all, if the public stops buying GM vehicles, the services of the assembly-line workers aren't as valuable. The simple answer, of course, is that the assembly-line worker doesn't want his contract contingent on the overall profitability of the company; he wants to be paid—and to get his pension and other benefits should he retire or quit—whether or not the company's stock does well. If it's acceptable for the assembly-line workers, why not for the CEO too?

A CEO Should Be Paid Well If a Company Does Well

Naturally, there is one obvious difference in this respect between assembly-line workers (or janitors and receptionists) and CEOs: Far more so than these other employees, the CEO can greatly influence the profitability of the company. Rather than giving the CEO a well-specified set of instructions to mechanically implement, the people hiring him allow far more discretion. After all, the CEO is brought in to run the company.

Yet this difference shows up quite clearly in the market: CEOs and other executives do get paid according to how well the company does. In addition to a base salary, these executives are often paid in stock options. A stock option (specifically a calf) gives its owner the right to purchase shares of stock at a specific price, called the strike price. Therefore, if the actual market price of the stock is lower than the strike price, the option is worthless. But if, through their behavior, executives can boost the company's stock price above the strike price, the options are valuable in proportion to the difference between the strike and actual prices.

Given his outrage over executives being paid regardless of profitability, one would expect Crowley to be a huge advocate of paying CEOs in nothing but stock options, which perfectly tailor earnings to the success of the company. Yet Crowley complains about the fairness of this too, even with highly successful companies. He cites the case of Yahoo! CEO Terry Semel, who took advantage of $230 million in stock options in 2004:

> The average Joe might be more outraged if he understood the sorts of payouts and benefits that corporate brass are getting. Stock grants still provide a windfall for many chief executives, despite new regulations that force companies to account for options as expenses. Yahoo! CEO Terry Semel exercised $230 million in options last year. His company has

had strong earnings of late so it's fair to say that Semel earned his $600,000 salary, plus a hefty award for boosting the stock price. But $230 million? Come on.

Now what exactly is Crowley's definition of fairness? If Semel is paid a large chunk of options, and under his leadership Yahoo! stock rises tremendously, why shouldn't he be rewarded in proportion to this gain? At this point we can see past Crowley's other alleged arguments; his basic objection is obviously that $230 million is more than anyone should earn, period.

Corporate Leadership and Performance Will Suffer If Pay Is Limited

There are three problems with this popular view. First, the upper limit that "decency" allows is arbitrary; no doubt many people would also deny the fairness of Semel's $600,000 base salary. ("We've got starving children in the streets and some guy who heads a company of spammers gets 600 grand a year?!")

Second, we must accept that in the modern economy, with billions of potential consumers worldwide, certain individuals have extraordinary earning power on the open market. If someone like Semel (or, a stronger case, Bill Gates) can add hundreds of millions of dollars of value to an organization (as judged by the spending habits of consumers), then to not pay him accordingly just means that someone else gets the money. Whatever happened to the principle of labor being paid the full value of its product? If Semel only got, say, $1 million, then Yahoo! shareholders (a group hardly in need of charity) would be $229 million richer. Would this outcome be fairer than what actually happened?

Third, we must consider the problem of incentives. If certain market exchanges are prevented because people such as Crowley find them unconscionable, then the individuals involved may stop working as much or as hard. For example, if Semel knew that outsiders would confiscate his stock options if the stock price rose too much, then he wouldn't have put in the long hours and sleepless nights that he undoubtedly did during the year in question.

This is a point liable to misinterpretation, and it's probably easier to switch contexts to professional sports. Economics tells us that placing a limit of, say, $1 million on salaries would reduce the incentives for star athletes. Now the critic might scoff and say, "Come on! Whether they make $1 million or $30 million, people will still go into the NBA [National Basketball Association]. That type of cap isn't going to affect anybody's career choice." Yet this objection overlooks the marginal nature of economic decisions. Yes, a first-round draft choice will still go pro (rather than become an accountant) even with a $1 million cap. But he'll probably retire much earlier. (In the extreme, consider the heavyweight champion of the world—once he earns his title, he won't defend it nearly as often if people like Crowley get to dismiss multimillion-dollar payments as unfairly high.)

This reasoning applies even more so to leadership positions in large companies. Especially when considered in the aggregate, if "outrageous" compensation packages are forbidden, the quality of corporate leadership will suffer. These people aren't qualified for just CEO spots, and they're well aware of the social stigma against big business. If the compensation packages are as high as they are, it's because that's what firms need to offer to attract and retain these highly skilled individuals. Of course, this phenomenon isn't peculiar to corporate-leadership positions; if we declared tomorrow that brain surgeons could only make 50 percent of their current salaries, the frequency and quality of brain surgery would plummet.

Cost-Cutting Will Not Result in More Money for the Shareholder

Of course, any reader who has actually worked in (or owns stock in) a large corporation may reject the above description as naive. In the real world, such a reader might object, most shareholders in practice exercise no control over management. Suppose, for example, that 85 percent of the shareholders (consisting of thousands of people who each owned far less than 1 percent of the stock) thought the CEO made far too much money. Even so, would it really be worth it for them to organize and demand that the corporate board do something? After all, the increased dividends made possible by such cost-cutting wouldn't translate into very much per shareholder. In this environment, management becomes entrenched and a lavish corporate culture takes over, with kept board members approving the jet-setting lifestyle of the CEO and his cronies.

As some of the recent scandals suggest, there definitely seems to be at least a grain of truth in such claims. Yet it nonetheless remains a puzzle to the free-market economist. For even if individual shareholders wouldn't find it worthwhile to organize and put an end to profligate abuses by management, such waste would nonetheless show up in the stock price of the firm. If, for example, management collectively frittered away $10 million per year in unjustifiable expenses, the total shares of the corporation would be valued around $200 million less than they otherwise would be, assuming an efficient stock market and an interest rate of 5 percent. (This is because $200 million is the present discounted value of a perpetual stream of $10 million annual dividends.) Such a corporation would then be a prime target for the much reviled corporate raider. The raider would institute a "hostile takeover," in which he bought up a controlling share in the corporation (by offering far more than the current price per share to the stockholders) and then used his power to fire or straighten out the inefficient managers. After cleaning house the corporation's dividends and/or stock price would rise accordingly, netting the raider a profit.

Thus we see that in the free market, even the realistic problems with "democratic" mechanisms can always be overcome in the final analysis by a "strongman," i.e. the corporate raider. (It should go without saying that these political metaphors are just that; in a free market all transactions are voluntary exchanges of property.) Consequently, if CEOs and other members of upper management make incredibly high earnings year after year, it must be that the shareholders find their services worth the expense. In some cases it may take the outside analyst some effort to discover how, but we shouldn't doubt that the shareholders are careful with their money.

Unfortunately, I cannot close the analysis on this optimistic note. For the above relies on the assumption of a free market in corporate takeovers, and that is decidedly lacking. In the present legal and cultural environment, so-called corporate raiders are even more despised than golden-parachuting CEOs. Regulations severely restrict so-called hostile takeovers, and hence hamper the ability of shareholders to restrain their managers. For example, the federal Williams Act (1968) compels a would-be raider to declare his intentions after acquiring 5 percent of a corporation's shares. Declaring one's intention to take over a company would likely push up the stock price, making the takeover plan unfeasible.

[I]f CEOs and other members of upper management make incredibly high earnings year after year, it must be that the shareholders find their services worth the expense.

The market's other checks on inefficient management are stifled as well. After all, even before the financial innovations allowing the issue of "junk bonds" and hostile takeovers, there was always a sure-fire way to keep corporate officers in line: any firm that wasted too much money on fancy offices and executive perks would be vulnerable to its competitors. Again, this initially poses a puzzle for critics such as Crowley; if outrageous compensation for CEOs is so endemic in American corporate culture, why don't new firms enter these industries and drive the old ones out of business?

But as with hostile takeovers, so too with new entrants to industry: Government regulation muffles this threat and thus allows entrenched businesses a margin of profligacy that they otherwise would not enjoy. Many people (especially young students) new to the ideas of laissez faire believe that big business opposes government meddling, but this is naïve and contradicted by the history of actual legislation. Ironically, the profitability of big business can actually be enhanced when the government regulates an industry, because the big firms can more easily handle the fixed costs of filling out paperwork, providing a "safe" working environment, proving that they are making every effort to comply with affirmative action goals, and so on. In this environment, would-be competitors face additional hurdles if they want to challenge the large incumbents, and thus the latter may indeed get away with lavish expenditures that would be short-lived in a truly free market.

> In the opinion of the demagogues inequality in what they call the "distribution" of wealth and incomes is in itself the worst of all evils. Justice would require an equal distribution. It is therefore both fair and expedient to confiscate the surplus of the rich or at least a considerable part of it and to give it to those who own less. This philosophy tacitly presupposes that such a policy will not impair the total quantity produced. But even if this were true, the amount added to the average man's buying power would be much smaller than extravagant popular illusions assume. In fact the luxury of the rich absorbs only a slight fraction of the nation's total consumption. The much greater part of the rich men's incomes is not spent for consumption, but saved and invested. It is precisely this that accounts for the accumulation of their 5 great fortunes. If the funds which the successful businessmen would have ploughed back into productive employments are used by the state for current expenditure or given to people who consume them, the further accumu-

lation of capital is slowed down or entirely stopped. Then there is no longer any question of economic improvement, technological progress, and a trend toward higher average standards of living.

—Ludwig von Mises, "Inequality of Wealth and Incomes"

6

Executives' High Salaries Should Be Capped

Dean Calbreath

Dean Calbreath writes a weekly column on business issues for the San Diego Union-Tribune *and also covers the economy, finance, and international trade for the* Union-Tribune.

There's a great deal of hostility and opposition to President Barack Obama's decision to put a limit of $500,000 on the salaries of executives who work for financial corporations seeking government assistance. However, these same opponents have no problem calling for middle- and working-class people to suffer with fewer working hours and pay cuts. Companies, such as Hewlett-Packard, have watched their stock drop and laid-off workers as a result, while still giving their CEOs a more-than-generous compensation package. There's a huge difference between how the poor and wealthy are dealt with in this country: The poor can earn only so much in order to apply for Medicaid, welfare, or food stamps, but many find it inappropriate to ask some executives not to make more than $500,000.

As the nation's jobless rate surges toward the 8 percent mark [in February 2009], with nearly 5 million people in unemployment lines, there seems to be a double standard for how some people view workers on Wall Street versus Main Street.

Throughout the nation, working-class stiffs are being asked to scale back their spending, work fewer hours and take daunting pay cuts—assuming that they're lucky enough to keep their jobs.

In California, most state government workers are being furloughed for two days per month, resulting in a 10 percent drop in their salaries. A growing number of private companies, including *The San Diego Union-Tribune*, are making similar cutbacks (temporarily, we hope).

Throughout the nation, working-class stiffs are being asked to scale back their spending, work fewer hours and take daunting pay cuts—assuming that they're lucky enough to keep their jobs.

The Average Worker Is Expected to Take a Pay Cut, but Not a CEO

Yet when it comes to the former Masters of the Universe on Wall Street—many of whom helped engineer the gigantic mess in which we find ourselves—there are still those who question President Barack Obama's decision last week to impose a $500,000 limit on executive salaries at the financial institutions looking to receive government aid.

Former Treasury Secretary Paul O'Neill called the cap "a huge mistake." Carly Fiorina, the former Hewlett-Packard chief executive who was Sen. John McCain's economics consultant last year, objected to the cap since "the opportunity to be rewarded for taking prudent risk is fundamental to our economic vitality and strength."

Scott Talbott, a lobbyist with the Financial Services Roundtable, said salaries should be allowed to reflect the executives' value on the open market.

"I don't think the issue is a dollar amount," Talbott told ABC News. "It's being paid what you're worth. Would you be willing to work for less than what you think you're worth?" (Note to Talbott: Exactly how many non-Wall Streeters have you asked that question?)

Bear in mind that Obama's restriction has a few major loopholes that will allow most executives to rake in far more than the $500,000 cap. For instance, it places no limits on how many stock options the companies can give their executives—the chief form of compensation these days—though it does impose some restrictions on when the options can be cashed in.

"Theoretically, you could give the executives $100 million worth of free shares," said Graef Crystal, a compensation analyst based in Santa Rosa.

In addition, the $500,000 limit is not retroactive and applies only to firms that are seeking money from the government. If a company is not getting a huge amount of money, it can request a waiver so it can pay its executives more. And it limits bonuses only for a company's most senior executives, such as the chief executive and chief financial officer.

"It's toothless," Crystal said. "What was it that Shakespeare said? A lot of 'sound and fury, signifying nothing.'"

Brian Foley, a compensation specialist in White Plains, N.Y., said that despite all "the moaning and groaning" about the cap, it would not have affected much of the $20 billion in bonuses given out on Wall Street last year—a major focal point of Obama's ire—because a large chunk of the bonuses went to lower-ranking executives, rather than the upper tier the White House targeted.

What is interesting is the double standard when it comes to how we treat our richest citizens versus what we pay our poorest.

The Rich and the Poor Are Treated Very Differently

We have no compunction in setting income limits on people applying for food stamps, welfare or Medicaid. But when we are asked to spend hundreds of billions of dollars helping Wall Street firms—some of which arguably should have been allowed to go bankrupt—we get a little skittish about asking people to limit their salaries to $500,000. (Frankly, I'd love to limit my salary to $500,000, but that would require a bit of upward movement beforehand.)

This difference also was apparent in the way Washington treated Wall Street and Detroit when both came, hat in hand, begging for money.

> *We have no compunction in setting income limits on people applying for food stamps, welfare or Medicaid. But when we are asked to spend hundreds of billions of dollars helping Wall Street firms ... we get a little skittish about asking people to limit their salaries to $500,000.*

When Wall Street asked for money last year, then-Treasury Secretary Hank Paulson, a former Wall Streeter, balked at imposing any requirements on executive pay or bonuses—or any requirements on how they spent the $700 billion bailout he engineered for them.

Six months later, we still don't know what all our money was spent on, though we do know that some money went to such things as buying a corporate jet, sending dividends to shareholders and providing billions of dollars' worth of bonuses to executives.

Compare that with how the automakers were treated. Washington refused to lend any money to the Detroit companies without demanding concessions from the unions, arm-twisting them to slim their salaries (far below the salaries of second-year stockbrokers at Lehman Brothers) and stop paying for health care for retired workers.

Whether those automaker salaries should have been lowered is a matter of debate. The unionized workers in Detroit now make roughly the same as nonunionized workers at Toyota plants in Kentucky, so it's not like they are heavily overpaid.

The point is not to say that Detroit should have gotten money without strings attached. But the difference in the way the factory workers and the financiers were treated is astounding.

In 1964, the average chief executive's salary was 24 times the average salary of workers within their companies. Today, it is estimated to be between 275 and 430 times the average, depending on who's counting.

Then again, the problem of unbridled executive pay is not limited to Wall Street.

Over the past 40 years—and especially in the past decade [2000-2010]—there has been a tremendous explosion in executive pay in this country. In 1964, the average chief executive's salary was 24 times the average salary of workers within their companies. Today, it is estimated to be between 275 and 430 times the average, depending on who's counting.

Over the past decade [2000-2010], executive salaries have risen five times faster than the average worker's.

"There's no question that salaries have gone out of whack—and that there's been an incredible gap between the compensation of the average worker and top executives," said Bill Sannwald, a management professor at San Diego State University.

CEOs' Salaries Rise No Matter What

On Main Street as well as Wall Street, these salaries have often risen no matter what the economic circumstances or the trajectory of the company's stock price.

Just last week [February 2, 2009], Hewlett-Packard disclosed that it had granted its chief executive $34 million in compensation last year [2008]—despite the fact that its stock dropped 25 percent over the past year, forcing around 25,000 layoffs. Walt Disney's chief executive received $51 million in compensation even as the firm acknowledged that the recession was cutting into its profits.

"I have not seen any indication that anybody's cutting back those salaries," compensation analyst Crystal said. "Giving somebody a $34 million salary during times like these does not seem to show a great deal of sensitivity."

Here in San Diego County—home to small and midsize companies—the salaries are not quite at Disney level, but they can be high. Compensation for top executives at Qualcomm has topped $6 million per year including salary and bonuses, while Sempra Energy compensation has risen to $4 million, Crystal said.

As the economy worsens, it seems likely that companies will start paring executive compensation—and the impetus will come from their boards of directors rather than Washington.

"I expect to see companies where bonuses are eliminated or substantially reduced, or where the board becomes a lot more judicious about who gets stock options and how much they get," compensation specialist Foley said. "The boards will have to be more sensitive about how their compensation appears to their workers, their shareholders, politicians and the media."

7

Executives' High Salaries Should Not Be Capped

Steven Pearlstein

Steven Pearlstein won the 2008 Pulitzer Prize for commentary.

Using salary caps as a way to limit the excessive compensation earned by executives in the financial sector is, at best, an unrealistic tool. There are too many other factors at work that make this approach unworkable. Unlike other businesses, there is less competition in the financial-services industry, so they will reap greater profits. The federal government also helps to ensure these companies' profits by allowing them tax breaks. As soon as the companies that borrowed money from the government repay that money, high salaries and generous compensation packages will once again return.

The rest of the country may be stuck in a nasty recession, but on Wall Street, where it all began, business is booming.

This week [July 2009], Goldman Sachs reported a record profit for the latest quarter while J.P. Morgan Chase weighed in with record revenue, and other banks are set to exceed expectations. Compensation levels in some areas are returning to 2007 levels, and firms are once again offering big salaries and guaranteed bonuses to lure away top traders and investment bankers.

Good news or bad?

Certainly we're all better off now that some banks are healthy enough to remove themselves from government life support and pay back the Treasury loans. And if well-run banks can again earn an honest profit by taking smart risks and restoring the flow of capital into the markets—well, that's what capitalism is all about.

The real problem with Wall Street pay is that these firms simply make too much money relative to the economic value they create.

Then again, it seems outrageous that the geniuses whose excessive risk-taking brought on the crisis, and who had to be bailed out by the rest of us, are the first to recover and could soon be earning what they did before.

It's the pay, of course, that gets everyone up in arms. Most firms are already revamping their compensation strategies to require that bonuses be earned over the long run. However effective this restructuring proves to be at dampening excessive risk-taking, it probably won't reduce overall pay, which explains why Wall Street has been so quick to embrace it. The real problem with Wall Street pay is that these firms simply make too much money relative to the economic value they create.

Less Competition Means Bigger Profits

If other industries were to enjoy such excessive profits, these would be eroded fairly quickly by competition as firms sought to increase market share by cutting prices. But in many segments of the financial services industry—investment banking being the best example—a natural oligopoly [a situation where a small number of companies dominate a market] has developed in which a relatively small number of blue-chip firms dominate the market. These firms compete fiercely against one another in every way except price, which allows them to earn those extraordinary profits.

There are several reasons for this less-than-perfect competition.

The most obvious is that, in this market, the relative reputation of the firm matters a whole lot more than price. If your company is floating a $10 billion bond issue, having a dependable lead underwriter sends a signal to most investors that you are a borrower who can be trusted, and so it's worth paying an extra $10 million to get Goldman Sachs to do it. Or if your company is trying to fend off a hostile takeover by General Electric, you probably are willing to pay a premium to get Bruce Wasserstein as your investment banker. There may well be banks or bankers just as smart and capable as Goldman and Wasserstein who would do the job for less. But getting it wrong could prove very costly.

Larger Companies Have an Advantage

This is also an industry in which size and scope matter a lot, meaning that the largest players have a big advantage. At Goldman Sachs and J.P. Morgan, for example, much of last quarter's profits were made by trading desks that bought and sold huge quantities of stocks, bonds, commodities, derivatives and other securities for their customers, as well as for their own accounts. Because so many trades pass through their hands, these large trading desks have the best real-time information about where markets are heading than anyone in the world, and they use that information to great competitive advantage—not only earning a little more than everyone else on each trade, but learning when to get into and out of markets.

Being big and having a good reputation don't guarantee success on Wall Street—just ask Lehman Brothers, Bear Stearns and Merrill Lynch—but they surely help. That's why a Wal-Mart hasn't emerged and crashed the Wall Street party by offering lower prices. In fact, what new entrants there are tend to be boutique firms started by industry superstars who trumpet their superior skills by charging more than the industry norm.

There is one other reason for Wall Street's extraordinary profits—the safety net provided by the federal government. Most firms would have to pay a considerable amount of money to ensure a reliable source of liquidity in the midst of a financial crisis. But as a practical reality, big banks and financial houses have always gotten their liquidity backstop at a huge discount, courtesy of the U.S. taxpayer.

Just because an industry earns outsize profits, of course, doesn't mean that those profits will necessarily go to employees in the form of outsize compensation. But that is often the case. That's what happened in the auto and steel industries in the 1960s, when unions successfully captured most of those industries' profits. It also happened at nonunion companies such as IBM and Microsoft, in the form of stock options and above-average pay.

In truth, the best way to restrain Wall Street pay is to restrain Wall Street's profits, either by increasing taxes, reducing leverage or inducing more robust competition. Trying to cap industry pay is like trying to cap a volcano.

Higher Salaries to Keep Everyone Happy

On Wall Street, much of the surplus is captured by superstar bankers and traders who generate a disproportionate share of those outsize profits, just as superstar actors have done in the movie business or superstar athletes in professional sports. And because these superstars work side by side with colleagues with similar skills doing similar work, firms tend to offer higher-than-market pay to everyone else to assure a modicum of workplace harmony.

For a brief moment, the financial crisis interrupted this compensation arms race as profits dried up. But now that profits are returning, there is no reason to believe that the inflated pay packages won't be far behind. Because the government's pay caps apply only to the firms that have been unable to pay back their loans from the Treasury, the effect of these rules won't be to reduce pay levels at Goldman Sachs or J.P. Morgan, but to weaken the weakest firms even further as their top talent is lured away.

In truth, the best way to restrain Wall Street pay is to restrain Wall Street's profits, either by increasing taxes, reducing leverage or inducing more robust competition. Trying to cap industry pay is like trying to cap a volcano.

8

Government Should Regulate Private-Sector Executive Compensation

Sarah Anderson and Sam Pizzigati

Sarah Anderson, the global economy project director at the Institute for Policy Studies, coauthored Field Guide to the Global Economy *and* Alternatives to Economic Globalization: A Better World Is Possible. *Sam Pizzigati, an associate editor at the Institute for Policy Studies, writes an online weekly column called "Too Much."*

President Barack Obama's proposal to limit executive salaries to $500,000 is, at best, a symbolic gesture; the cap will only apply to those companies who accept government assistance. Instead, a national pay standard should be adopted that adheres to a ratio of 25 to 1 for the difference between an executive's salary and the salary of the company's lowest-paid worker. Some will argue that it is not the government's place to set restrictions on the actions of a private corporation. Limiting an executive's salary, however, is just as necessary as, and equivalent to, the kind of restrictions that ban companies from putting dangerous chemicals in products.

In his first week as president, Barack Obama cited years of "greed and irresponsibility on the part of some" as a major contributing factor behind our economic meltdown. In his second week, he denounced Wall Street's latest round of multibillion-dollar bonuses as "shameful." In his third week, he proposed what amounts to a "maximum wage," a $500,000 cap that would apply to at least a few banking executives lining up for a share of the exceptionally large TARP [Troubled Asset Relief Program] bailout.

So what can we expect for an encore? When he announced his executive wage cap, Obama gave us a clue. The president promised to launch a special "long-term effort" to examine "broader reforms" around executive pay.

Presidents typically convene such "long-term efforts" to kick the public policy can down the road until an energized public loses interest. Let's hope this one proves different. We desperately need a sober, thoughtful review that can get us past the muddled clichés that dominate the CEO pay debate.

"Lavish bonuses," Obama noted, are enabling a "culture of narrow self-interest and short-term gain at the expense of everything else."

Obama's remarks so far, unfortunately, have done precious little to clear up matters. At one point in his announcement, he seemed to swallow whole the conventional take that stratospheric pay levels are just fine as long as executives are meeting the criteria for performance "success" as corporate boards so narrowly define them. "This is America," Obama observed. "We believe that success should be rewarded. But what gets people upset—and rightfully so—are executives being rewarded for failure."

Excessive Executive Pay Has Contributed to the Economy's Downfall

But other comments by the president hint at a much deeper understanding of the danger inherent in the enormous rewards that have metastasized across corporate America. "Lavish bonuses," Obama noted, are enabling a "culture of narrow self-interest and short-term gain at the expense of everything else." Executive pay excesses "have contributed to a reckless culture and quarter-by-quarter mentality that in turn have wrought havoc in our financial system."

So what should we be battling: rewards for CEO "failure" or "lavish bonuses"? The answer makes a difference.

If the problem does boil down to paying for failure, then we ought to empower shareholders. Give them a "say on pay"—the right to take advisory votes on executive pay packages—and, mainstream reformers claim, corporate boards will end their wasteful ways.

In reality, we mandate limits on corporate behavior all the time. . . . We set these limits because we recognize that irresponsible corporate behaviors threaten our communities.

The Cap on Salary Doesn't Go Far Enough

But if the problem revolves around the size of the rewards, then the solution demands more robust government action. Obama's $500,000 cap moves us a tiny, mostly symbolic step forward. Gaping loopholes abound. The cap applies only to failing firms that in the future will receive vaguely defined "exceptional assistance." And even these few firms will be able to reward top execs with unlimited millions in restricted stock they can claim once the firms repay the government. Shouldn't the rewards go first and foremost to the taxpayers, who are bankrolling recovery?

We still, in short, have plenty of work to do to end bailout profiteering. Apologists for our corporate order, naturally, will howl if the administration dares to do it. In a "free society," they'll fume, government has no right to place limits on private corporate behavior, no right to "dictate" how much corporations pay their power suits.

In reality, we mandate limits on corporate behavior all the time. We limit how much pollution corporations can spew out. We limit the chemicals companies can sneak into their products. We limit the hours they can force employees to labor. We set these limits because we recognize that irresponsible corporate behaviors threaten our communities.

Excessive executive pay, the Wall Street meltdown has demonstrated ever so vividly, endangers our public well-being as surely as any pollutant. Jackpots have become so huge that executives will do anything to hit them. They'll even drive our economy into the ditch.

Most Americans seem to get it. That's why Senator Claire McCaskill of Missouri electrified the nation on January 30 [2009] by blasting the "idiots" of Wall Street and proposing a $400,000 pay cap at all bailed-out companies. The Senate, on a voice vote, adopted the proposal after McCaskill and Senator Bernie Sanders offered it as an amendment to the stimulus.

In 2007, big-time CEOs made 344 times what the average US worker took home.

Taxpayers Help to Subsidize CEO Salaries

This $400,000 equals the salary of President Obama, who's making about twenty-five times more than the government's lowest-paid worker. Peter Drucker, the founder of modern management science, considered twenty-five to one an appropriate ratio for the private sector as well. Larger gaps, he argued before his death four years ago [in 2005], undermine enterprise effectiveness and efficiency. In 2007, big-time CEOs made 344 times what the average US worker took home.

The twenty-five-to-one ratio ought to become our national pay standard, not just for bailed-out companies but for all enterprises that get government support, whether through contracts or subsidies or tax breaks. Last year [2008] Mark

Hurd, Hewlett-Packard's CEO, took home $42.5 million. HP's biggest subsidiary gets more than $2 billion a year in federal contracts. Our tax dollars are, in effect, subsidizing CEO pay windfalls.

How do we start reversing this outrage? California Representative Barbara Lee is pushing legislation that would cap the amount of executive compensation firms are permitted to deduct from their corporate income taxes at twenty-five times the pay of their lowest-paid worker. If that became law, corporations could opt to continue paying their top executives tens of millions of dollars a year. But they would have to find somebody other than taxpayers to help them foot the bill.

9

Government Should Not Regulate Private-Sector Executive Compensation

Mitchell Schnurman

Mitchell Schnurman, a columnist at the Fort Worth Star-Telegram *since 2001, has covered business news in North Texas since 1986.*

While the excessively high salaries and compensation packages of many executives might be considered a real problem, a more pressing issue facing the country is the need to revive the economy. Past attempts by the government to control exorbitant CEO salaries have resulted in even higher salaries and compensation packages. In addition, the notion of deciding how much pay is too much raises many complex questions that are not easily resolved.

As if it's not tough enough to bail out the banks and rescue the economy, we want to rein in executive pay, too? And wrap it up this weekend? Good luck with that. Late Friday [September 26, 2008], federal lawmakers were still working on a $700 billion plan to buy bad mortgage debt, free up the credit markets and save the financial system. Many politicos insisted that the rescue include a limit on executive pay at any company that gets a bailout, arguing that taxpayer money should not enrich some executives who helped create the mess in the first place. That's a reasonable stance and, in the minds

Mitchell Schnurman, "CEO Pay Is a Real Problem, but This Isn't the Time to Fix It," *Fort Worth Star-Telegram*, September 28, 2008. Copyright © 2008 by *Fort Worth Star-Telegram*. Reproduced by permission.

of many, it should set a precedent for broader reform. If only it would work. Twenty-five years ago, Congress tried to put a lid on golden parachutes with a special tax on payouts that topped three times annual pay. Rather than discourage the practice, corporate America saw the regulation as an endorsement, and hundreds of companies adopted the agreements for the first time. By 2000, 70 percent of the 1,000 largest companies had them, and the standard payout became—you guessed it—three times annual pay, just beneath the tax threshold. In 1994, Congress took another stab at curbing executive pay. Salaries that topped $1 million would no longer be tax-deductible, prompting companies to do two things: raise the standard base pay to $1 million and compensate executives with loads of stock options, which weren't subject to the tax hit.

In six years, the average CEO pay for the S&P 500 companies rose from $3.3 million to $14 million, according to a study led by Michael Jensen of Harvard Business School. And options accounted for most of the surge, helped by both the new pay plans and a roaring stock market.

Regulation Often Makes Things Worse

This experience says a lot about the unintended consequences of regulation. It also shows that companies almost always find a way to keep paying top performers, regardless of the public reaction. Today, many large companies even cover the added taxes on executive benefits, ensuring that leaders net what they've been promised. So while government caps may boost taxes for the federal Treasury, they've added an accelerant to CEO compensation. By the way, I haven't heard any calls to limit Tony Romo's salary or Nicole Kidman's $20 million take on a film. How about Jerry Jones' $1 billion gain from owning the Dallas Cowboys for the past 20 years? They're not seeking a government rescue, of course, but the backlash on executive pay predates the current financial crisis. Now the reformers figure they have the leverage to do something. In my view, something needs to be done—but the timing couldn't be much worse. Rescuing the financial system is Crisis No. 1, and by comparison, curbing executive pay is a sideshow. Dan Short, an accounting professor at Texas Christian University [TCU], says it's like going to put out a house fire and having to also deal with complaints about how the owners treat the neighbors or take care of the yard. "We have to put out the fire—that is, stabilize the financial markets, and everything else is almost irrelevant," Short says. "If we throw executive compensation into it, it's going to be done wrong." Short, too, believes the executive pay system is broken in the United States. There's not enough accountability and not enough shareholder power in curbing the excesses.

"But I'd like to keep the government out of it," says Short, the former dean of TCU's Neeley School of Business. My problem is how to define "excessive" pay. Isn't that in the eye of the beholder?

Rescuing the financial system is Crisis No. 1, and by comparison, curbing executive pay is a sideshow.

How Do You Decide What Is Excessive?

In North Texas, XTO Energy's Bob Simpson was paid almost $60 million in each of the past two years, and complaints were relatively muted, because the company's performance was stellar. Simpson has even been recognized as one of the world's best CEOs by Barron's. At American Airlines, CEO Gerard Arpey was vilified by his own employees, after his pay package totaled $6.6 million. That's roughly one-tenth the pay for Simpson, yet Arpey oversees an operation with four times the revenue and 83,000 more employees. Perhaps most important, XTO generated three times more profit last year. So whose pay is excessive? And how would government make that judgment? The rescue plan has been vague, with one proposal that golden parachutes be barred and the treasury secretary set the standards on excess. Another idea is to limit the maximum to $2 million a year. Yet another is to reduce the $1 million cap on corporate tax deductibility to $400,000, and include all payments—options, grants and other benefits. Still another proposes to limit the maximum to 25 times the annual wage of the lowest-paid worker; that standard was introduced in the early '90s in the House of Representatives and endorsed by Peter Drucker, the late management guru. If the lowest salary at a company is $50,000, that would translate into maximum pay of $1.25 million. CEOs in the financial industry got an average pay package of $18.8 million last year, although that was valued before many of their stock options went underwater.

Still, imagine what happens if executives are facing that kind of pay cut. Count on much of the top talent to switch industries or move into private equity, where they can get a healthy stake and a shot at a huge payday. Sarah Anderson of the Institute for Policy Studies, a Washington think tank, says that won't be a problem. "There are lots of talented people out there, who will be willing to step up," she says. Bob Dill, who's worked on executive compensation for the Hay Group in Dallas since 1983, isn't so sure. He says that directors are constantly wrestling with how to attract and retain top performers without going overboard. "The committees spend so much time on this, and there's no silver bullet," he says. Public disclosure is the best bet, in my opinion, along with giving shareholders the power to reject pay plans. Publicly traded companies must now reveal in-depth details about salaries, stock options and the like, providing a clearer picture of total compensation. That hasn't reversed the rise in executive pay, but it has put more emphasis on performance. And unlike some of the past government moves, it hasn't made things worse.

10

Shareholders Must Be Active in Determining Executive Compensation

Fred G. Steingraber and Karen Kane

Fred G. Steingraber is chairman and CEO emeritus of A.T. Kearney, a global operations consulting firm, and chairman of Board Advisors. He has served on 12 corporate boards and 17 not-for-profit boards. Karen Kane, former board secretary for the Federal Reserve Bank of Chicago, heads a communication practice providing independent communication counsel to boards.

Many blame the Wall Street financial disaster on the fact that corporate boards neglected to do their job in overseeing the way corporations do business, including the compensation received by executives. Boards must show that they are independent and self-governing in order to re-establish the confidence of shareholders. There are a number of factors that compensation boards should take into account while they restructure, including linking long-term company performance to executive compensation. Above all, compensation boards must stress accountability, objectivity, and transparency.

Financial regulation and shareholder activism are a direct response to the board's overly defensive posture and perceived dismissal of the shareholder's role in corporate governance. Congress, taxpayers, activist shareholders—and now a blockbuster book written by Wall Street insiders—blame the

Fred G. Steingraber and Karen Kane, "Boards Need to Regain High Ground and Preserve Relevance," *Directorship*, vol. 36, June/July 2010. Copyright © 2010 National Association of Corporate Directors. Reproduced by permission.

financial crisis on a systemic collapse of corporate democracy caused by the utter failure of corporate boards to do their jobs. In the last three years [2007–2010], directors have presided over corporate governance failures that cost shareholders trillions of dollars.

But will boards own up to their true responsibility and take on the considerable work required to bring true oversight to management? Recent regulatory action has endorsed shareholder legitimacy for holding boards accountable. With the [2010] annual meeting season in full swing, corporate boards need to assert their independence and autonomy in carrying out their role of governance while providing true oversight of corporations. Interestingly, the loudest critics of corporate boards do not advocate their elimination. Rather, they want boards to provide greater oversight by asserting their independence and doing the job for which they have been hired.

Boards Must Show Leadership

It will take substantive changes for boards to regain the trust needed to re-establish their governance authority. A board must thoughtfully reorganize itself, examine the competencies of its members as well as board processes and committee roles. Boards need to transform themselves into strong, highly functioning work groups whose members trust and challenge one another. Directors also need to recognize the role shareholders play: They are the owners of the company and board/shareholder engagement is an important element in keeping them invested. Most importantly, boards need to demonstrate leadership with a transparent, results-orientation in the conduct of their work.

No other entity can provide the oversight that an independent, engaged and committed board can deliver. We all have an enormous stake in reforming boards to carry out the responsibility for providing true oversight of management in a complex global business environment. Directors need to rethink and reconfigure their committee structure and committee work for greater effectiveness—which will likely involve a combination of some new responsibilities in existing committees, the creation of new committees and new skills and qualifications for directors.

In the future, boards must also include greater committee work on leadership development and succession planning, operations, growth, risk management and shareholder communication if they hope to provide meaningful and credible oversight for the companies they represent.

Change the Way Boards Work

As in all blueprints for change, the devil is in the details. The following ideas represent a fundamental shift in the breadth and focus of board work required, which will bring about other needed changes. As boards get back to the proper oversight of management and focus on leadership development, corporate strategy, corporate performance and risk management, the enterprise itself will be strengthened.

The following is an outline of the responsibilities, roles and skills which need to be addressed in new or existing committees more effectively:

Leadership development/succession planning: Boards need to spend far more time in this area, including overseeing the human resource alignment with the business strategy. The issue of leadership development and succession is without a doubt the area of highest risk if not pursued in a proactive mode by the board of directors.

Operations to include the establishment of performance targets by implementing best practices in productivity, quality and service. In addition, boards should audit the application of technology, shared services and outsourcing to achieve performance improvement. Such audits provide a vital forward-looking area of key indicators impacting risk and future financial performance.

Corporate growth and resources to include reviewing organic growth targets and trends. This should include products and services, markets and channels, geography and relevant resource requirements to achieve and sustain growth. This committee should oversee the due diligence related to acquisitions as well as post-merger audits. They would also be responsible for understanding and overseeing the targeted and actual growth in revenues from new products in the last three to five years.

A risk management committee should be configured to oversee issues which can affect the business, including macro-economic conditions, regulatory trends, demographic changes, technology, competition, environment, consumer behavior, energy, leadership depth and breadth, financial resources and balancing change and continuity. In addition, this committee should periodically review a strength, weakness, opportunity and threat analysis (SWOT).

Shareholder communications requires a more proactive approach to transparency across multiple audiences—including investors, brokers, and owner research groups—as well as through traditional outlets such as proxies, annual reports and on investor website portals.

Incentive compensation awards for executives should be tied to the long-term business performance and not share price. While goals may include both short- and long-term targets, longer-term performance and goals should be weighted more heavily.

Tie Compensation to Long-Term Goals

Compensation committees should adopt a clear statement of compensation philosophy, which provides a transparent understanding of the factors that drive compensation decisions. Incentive compensation awards for executives should be tied to the long-term business performance and not share price. While goals may include both short- and long-term targets, longer-term performance and goals should be weighted more heavily.

Perhaps of greatest importance is the need to move to a principles-based system of compensation determination and reporting. Examples of key principles could include accountability, alignment, fairness, transparency and objectivity. Accountability should demonstrate that incentive pay is tied to business-performance targets and metrics based on audited financial results and clawbacks for earnings restatements or fraud. The principle of alignment should address CEO incentive compensation in relation to shareholder rewards and incentives for other top-level executives and tying it to longer-term business performance with incentive compensation to include a deferred component. Executives should be required to hold a targeted level of share investment in relationship to their compensation. . . . Objectivity should be demonstrated through verification of the independence of all compensation committee members and compensation consultants. Finally, transparency should be demonstrated by communicating clearly both internally and externally the company's compensation principles, the application thereof and, if not, why not, and what has been done instead.

Objectivity should be demonstrated through verification of the independence of all compensation committee members and compensation consultants.

Lastly, boards need to carefully consider some of the new skills and qualifications required of directors to carry out the responsibilities outlined above. Boards will need to recruit beyond sitting CEOs to academicians, human resource executives, research leaders and experts in competitive assessment and shareholder communications.

In this new world, directors will need to engage with a broader group of stakeholders, convincing them of the board's execution of their duty of loyalty and duty of care in overseeing the enterprise.

11

Executives Put Profits Before Good Business Decisions

Les Leopold

Les Leopold is the executive director of the Labor Institute and the Public Health Institute in New York. He wrote The Looting of America: How Wall Street's Game of Fantasy Finance Destroyed Our Jobs, Pensions and Prosperity and What We Can Do About It.

Wall Street is responsible for the fiscal mess facing the country because the financial industry puts profits above sound business practices. Deregulating financial services and changing the tax code to benefit the wealthy contributed to the problem. Such collateralized debt obligations (CDOs) as junk bonds, auto loans, and subprime loans made Wall Street a lot of money, but everything collapsed when increasingly indebted consumers could no longer afford to pay off their debts. The average American suffered, while Wall Street was given loans and Troubled Asset Relief Program (TARP) funds. The government must do more to protect Americans, including banning future collateralized debt obligations.

Morgan Stanley plans to repackage a downgraded collateralized debt obligation backed by leveraged loans into new securities with AAA ratings in the first transaction of its kind, said two people familiar with the sale. Morgan Stanley is selling $87.1 million of securities that it expects to

Les Leopold, "Wall Street's Gall," *The Progressive*, vol. 73, no. 9, September 2009. Copyright © 2009 by *The Progressive*. Reproduced by permission of *The Progressive*, 409 East Main Street, Madison, WI 53703, www.progressive.org.

receive top AAA ratings and $42.9 million of notes graded Baa2, the second lowest investment grade by Moody's Investors Service.

—Bloomberg News, *July 8, 2009*

You've got to admire their gall. Wall Street firms crashed the entire world economy by selling fantasy finance instruments. They got bailed out by us to the tune of trillions of dollars in TARP [Troubled Asset Relief Program] money, cheap loans, and asset guarantees. And then they take our money and start it all over again!

And nobody in a position to do so seems willing to stop them.

Actually, the story is so outrageous that Wall Street is counting on us not to believe it.

Wall Street firms crashed the entire world economy by selling fantasy finance instruments. They got bailed out by us to the tune of trillions of dollars in TARP money, cheap loans, and asset guarantees. And then they take our money and start it all over again!

Deregulation and Reforming the Tax Code Resulted in Disaster

Let's take it from the top. Starting in the late 1970s, the nation embarked on a grand experiment. Our leading economists and policy makers believed heart and soul that our economy truly could become magnificent if we did two things: 1) deregulate financial services as much as possible; and 2) "reform" the tax code so that the wealthiest among us would be unshackled to create new and wondrous investments and products for our economy. These steps (along with demolishing unions, gutting the minimum wage, and running pell-mell toward globalization) were to bring about an investment boom of mammoth proportions throughout our economy, and so raise all boats.

The yachts sure did rise. Here are some statistics:

* In 1970, the ratio of the top 100 corporate CEOs and the average worker's pay was 40 to 1. By 2007 it was 1,723 to 1.

* In 1970, the top 1 percent received 8 percent of the national income. By 2007, it was gobbling up 23 percent of the national income.

* In 2006, the top one-tenth of 1 percent of tax payers (about 1 40,000 tax returns) reported as much income as the bottom 50 percent (67.4 million tax returns). The last time we suffered from such an extreme income distribution? 1928–29.

Most of us had leaky boats. Between 1975 and 2007, the real wages of the average production worker (94 million of them, as of 2007) decreased by 18 percent.

So what did the tiny fraction do with all the money? Some of it was invested in the real economy. But there was so much money looking for tangible investments that opportunities dwindled along with rates of return. As a result, *The Wall Street Journal* noted four years ago [in 2005], "Global investors are diving into a wide range of riskier assets: emerging countries' stocks and bonds; real estate and real estate-backed debt; commodity funds; fine art; private-equity funds, which buy stakes in nonpublic companies; and the investment contracts called derivatives, including a kind structured to permit the sophisticated to take huge bond risks."

Wall Street did what finance always does when income distributions get out of whack. It created a fantasy finance casino to attract that surplus capital.

Too Much Debt

Wall Street's hottest products were built around collateralized debt obligations (CDOs) and other derivatives, which Warren

Buffett has called "financial weapons of mass destruction." Investment alchemists turned subprime loans, junk bonds, and risky auto loans into AAA-rated securities. They sliced and diced vast pools of this debt into securities that had varying amounts of risks that corresponded with various rates of return. The more risk, the higher the rate of return. And all of the rates turned out to be higher than comparably rated plain vanilla corporate or government bonds. It was a miracle of financial innovation.

Elite investors, hungry for the higher returns, grabbed these new securities as fast as they could. And since each one contained enormous embedded fees for the top banks and investment houses that produced them, Wall Street grew fat and rich—richer than ever in the history of finance.

The demand for these new products grew so great that the supply of junk debt couldn't keep up with it. There just weren't enough subprime mortgages to feed the beast. So our financial engineers invented new securities. Rather than taking the time and expense to assemble new pools of junk debt, they used insurance policies, called credit default swaps, to make "synthetic" collateralized debt obligations. Again the rating agencies, which were (and still are) paid by the large financial institutions to rate their goodies, would bless most of the slices with AA and AAA ratings.

No credit, no jobs, no mortgage payments—and down we go. Welcome to the Great Depression II.

These new synthetic CDOs also sold briskly, which led to even more exotic inventions like CDOs squared and cubed. All of it was unregulated.

Some institutions, like AIG, decided they could make a killing if they insured the risky CDO investments of others from default. The more fantasy finance instruments they insured, the more premiums they received, and the more secure their counterparties felt having their CDO slices guaranteed against failure. What a felicitous confluence of interests. The consumer got access to more and more credit, the wealthy got higher rates of returns, and Wall Street got fat fees—and then bonuses that would have made the Pharaohs blush.

There was only one small problem. The underlying assets that propped up this entire house of cards were getting shakier and shakier. When housing prices shot through the roof, losing all contact with economic reality, our deeply indebted consumers could not possibly continue to increase their debt load. The inevitable happened. Prices stopped rising and then declined. Strapped homeowners fell behind on their payments. The asset values behind the loans declined. The value of CDOs formed from the pools of junk debt declined, as did the various offspring of the synthetic securities. Through the miracle of modern financial engineering (and old-time greed), trillions of dollars of securities turned toxic in a manner of months, crashing the world's financial system. Credit froze because every major financial institution was loaded with toxic assets and knew that others were in the same fix. They refused to loan to anyone. The freeze pushed the real economy off a cliff since nearly every business runs on credit. No credit, no jobs, no mortgage payments—and down we go. Welcome to the Great Depression II.

To reboot the system, Wall Street received trillions of dollars of loans, asset guarantees, and TARP funds almost overnight—the greatest transfer of wealth since slavery. Nomi Prins, the writer and former managing director at Goldman Sachs, calculates that Wall Street has sponged up over $13.3 trillion and counting.

Repaying Their Loans So They Can Go Back to Their Old Ways

Having put the entire financial sector on the dole, Congress suffered a momentary bout of populism and instituted wage caps on bankers at those institutions that received TARP funds. Needless to say, TARP recipients wanted to pay back the Treasury as rapidly as possible so that the elite bankers and traders could go back to high-flying compensation packages.

Morgan Stanley is among the first to break clear of TARP restrictions. On June 17 [2009], with much ballyhoo in the press, they paid back $10 billion to the Treasury. I'm sure many fine wines were cracked open that night. Whoopee! We're free of the $500,000 wage cap (which to Wall Street top executives is barely a subsistence wage). And since new financial regulations have not as yet been enacted, this is the perfect time to boost profits through a little casino CDO gambling.

Here's the hidden outrage to which Prins draws our attention: Even after the TARP repayments, Morgan Stanley still owes us nearly $25 billion. They are profiting mightily from the $23.7 billion "Temporary Liquidity Guarantee Program," which gives investors a big incentive to throw their money at the banks again because the government has them covered.

They should prohibit the creation of new collateralized debt obligations. They should outlaw the future securitization of mortgages. And they should insist that any financial instrument that serves as an insurance policy be strictly regulated, just like insurance is supposed to be.

So Morgan Stanley is once again peddling financial weapons of mass destruction. It is repackaging old toxic assets into new ones—and booking fat fees in the process. Apparently, they've also added a new layer of guarantees so that our trusty watchdog of financial probity—Moody's—will bless it with a AAA rating. But don't hold your breath thinking that you'll share in the spoils of this rich man's game. The public is subsidizing Morgan Stanley's experiment in gall, but the profits will stay squarely in Morgan Stanley's private pockets.

And just to rub it in so it really hurts: They're using their listener-supported funds to finance the lobbyists who are fighting any and all controls on their crap game, including the proposed Consumer Financial Protection Agency.

The Obama Administration and Congress have a golden opportunity to shut down this casino before the dice roll. They should prohibit the creation of new collateralized debt obligations. They should outlaw the future securitization of mortgages. And they should insist that any financial instrument that serves as an insurance policy be strictly regulated, just like insurance is supposed to be.

Wall Street is carefully watching this test. Will Obama, [Vice President Joe] Biden, [Director of the National Economic Council Lawrence] Summers, [US Secretary of the Treasury Timothy] Geithner, [Chairman of the Federal Reserve Ben] Bernanke, [Senator Chris] Dodd, or [Representative Barney] Frank do something, or just blink? Right now we've got a lot of fluttering eyelashes.

12

Government Regulation Is the Wrong Way to Fix Executive Compensation

Edward E. Lawler III

Edward E. Lawler III is Distinguished Professor of Business at the University of Southern California Marshall School of Business, and founder and director of the University's Center for Effective Organizations. His books include Talent: Making People Your Competitive Advantage.

Corporations accepting Troubled Asset Relief Program (TARP) funding have to cap their executives' salaries to $500,000. This action might result in greater regulation of executive salaries by the federal government. Government action might not have the desired effect. Rather, these factors should be kept in mind while attempting to control executive compensation packages: government regulation can put corporations at a disadvantage in hiring well-qualified people, who will simply go to a privately held company for more money; regulating what an executive can earn also will have a negative effect on job performance; and the average American might look more favorably on executives who make less money. How can boards better control compensation plans? One way is to ensure that the chair of the board is not part of (or has not been employed by) the corporation. Another way is to let the shareholders vote on the compensation plans for executives.

As a result of the executive pay cap in companies taking TARP funding, the door has been opened for increased federal regulation of executive compensation. It is impossible at this point to predict how open the door is and whether or not it is just the first step in an effort by the federal government to control executive compensation in the U.S. It could be the only action taken or the first of many actions that are triggered by growing public anger over the pay levels of senior executives.

This is not the first time that Congress has passed laws that attempt to regulate executive compensation. Indeed, perhaps the most comprehensive effort was the establishment of a wage and price control board during the inflation-ridden 1970s. This effort, like the ones that have followed, is generally considered to have been ineffective. No doubt they changed compensation practices and levels, but not necessarily in the intended way. Indeed, some have argued that past regulation efforts are partially responsible for the high levels of executive compensation that have resulted in today's demands for controls on executive compensation in the financial services industry and elsewhere.

In 1993, a change in the tax code limited the deductibility of CEO pay as a business expense. It means that corporations can treat only $1 million of salary as a business expense for each of its five top executives. Not covered by this provision are all kinds of incentive compensation (e.g., bonuses and stock). Most agree that the effect of this provision was to establish $1 million as the acceptable level of base salary for top executives. Further, it appears to have stimulated the development of the "pay for performance" plans that have contributed to the high level of executive compensation that exists today.

In 2006, the SEC issued a set of disclosure requirements for executive compensation that ordered companies to provide in "plain English" a view of their executive compensation plans. The result was to add long (often 30-plus pages) reports on compensation plans to proxy statements, but it did little if anything to change how and how much executives were paid.

Whenever regulations are proposed for executive compensation, the key question is whether they are likely to be effective. In order to answer this question we need to specify what we expect executive compensation to accomplish. Most research on executive compensation suggests that there are four ways an effective executive compensation plan can contribute to organizational effectiveness. It is important to look at each of these and examine whether government regulation of executive compensation is likely to increase the degree to which executive compensation plans support them.

The four are: control the cost of compensation, attract and retain the right executives, motivate the right executive performance and present the right optics concerning executive compensation to key organizational stakeholders. Each of these deserves separate attention, so let's look at them in turn.

Some have argued that past regulation efforts are partially responsible for the high levels of executive compensation that have resulted in today's demands for controls on executive compensation in the financial services industry and elsewhere.

Control the Cost of Executive Compensation

Executive compensation is a business expense, and as such it is appropriate to try to position it at a cost level that is "reasonable" and "competitive." There is good reason to believe that executive compensation in many U.S. corporations is too high by some reasonable standards. For example, there are some corporations that have pay levels that are out of line with the U.S. market for executive compensation and reduce corporate earnings accordingly. It is also true that executive pay levels in U.S.-based corporations are higher than those elsewhere in the world. This is particularly true in large corporations. As a result, U.S.-based corporations have higher executive salary costs than their offshore competitors.

Past regulations have led to greater use of stock, deferred compensation, golden parachutes and a host of other compensation programs. Still, it seems likely that the right regulations can lead to some decreases in executive compensation.

It is highly likely that federal regulation of executive compensation could reduce the total compensation of executives. Regardless of whether new regulations and laws increase the tax rate on high levels of compensation, simply forbid the issuing of paychecks above a certain amount or limit stock grants and stock options, it is likely that government intervention could to some degree reduce the amount of executive total compensation. It is also undoubtedly true that if regulations are put in, a great deal of effort will go into getting around them. Executives in most corporations have extensive corporate resources that they can use to assure that they get the maximum amount of compensation possible, given any regulations that are put in place to reduce their total compensation level. New perquisites are likely to appear, indirect forms of compensation will flourish and executive compensation consultants will have a field day proposing new compensation approaches that will get around whatever regulations or tax provisions are put into place.

At this point, without knowing the specifics of the regulations that might come into place it is impossible to know what approaches might be used to be sure that executives are highly compensated in the face of restrictions and regulations.

Past regulations have led to greater use of stock, deferred compensation, golden parachutes and a host of other compensation programs. Still, it seems likely that the right regulations can lead to some decreases in executive compensation.

Attract and Retain the Right Executives

Perhaps the most important thing that an effective executive compensation plan can do is to attract and retain the right executives. Attraction and retention are influenced by two features of any compensation package: its total amount and what forms of compensation are in it. Obviously, the higher total amount of compensation, the more attractive a compensation package is to an executive. The features of the plan—that is, whether it pays out in stock, cash, short term/long term, etc.— also have a big impact on attraction and retention. Deferred compensation and long-term pay plans can be powerful retention devices, although they may not be highly effective in recruiting senior executives. Stock options, stock grants and bonus plans can be particularly powerful retention devices if the company performs well.

For most companies, the key issue is finding the combination of base pay, incentive pay, stock and deterred compensation that will retain high-performing executives. Often, it is not simple to put together a package that appeals to the kind of high-performing executives companies want to employ. It takes a relatively complex mixture of current incentive compensation and long-term incentive compensation. This, in turn, requires cash and stock vehicles that are tied to the individual's performance as well as the company's performance. In short, packages often need to be complex and carefully designed. It is because of this that regulations are likely to be very counterproductive when it comes to attracting and retaining the right executives for most companies. They are likely to interfere with creating pay packages that can be fine-tuned and tailored to the attraction and retention needs of particular organizations and individuals. For example, they may make it impossible to pay the kind of attraction and retention bonuses that are needed to get key executives from other firms or to keep them from leaving. They also may make it very difficult to pay the market rate for key executives and to lock them in with deferred compensation.

Pay regulations are likely to be particularly dysfunctional with respect to attraction and retention when only certain industries or parts of industries are regulated. This, of course, is the condition that has been created by the TARP pay cap that was passed by Congress in February. It puts all companies that are subject to the cap at a tremendous competitive disadvantage with respect to attracting and retaining the best executives. They simply cannot compete with private equity companies, foreign companies, etc., for the best talent. As a result, the pay cap legislation is more likely to weaken the companies than to strengthen them at a time when their performance is key to the performance of the U.S. economy.

But what about a situation where all U.S. publicly traded corporations are regulated with respect to the level of executive compensation? This certainly is possible, and may seem like a good solution, but it doesn't solve the problem. With the many private companies and foreign companies that will not be limited in what they pay, there will be a brain drain from regulated companies to companies that for one reason or another do not fall under any government total compensation or pay package regulations.

Overall, the correct conclusion with respect to the effect of government regulations on executive compensation when it comes to attracting and retaining the right executives is that it will be more dysfunctional than functional. Perhaps the biggest concern is that it will put those companies that are regulated at a competitive disadvantage to those that are not when it comes to attracting and retaining the best executives. This could be particularly dysfunctional since regulations are likely to focus on the very large publicly traded corporations that are critical to the American economy.

Motivate Performance

Perhaps the most complicated area when it comes to executive compensation is motivation. In some respects, the way compensation affects motivation is relatively simple and straightforward. When all is said and done, individuals tend to be motivated to perform in a particular way when they are rewarded for performing in that way. How motivated they are is very much a function of how clear the connection is between performance and reward, and, of course, how large the reward for performance is. It is this very rationale that has led to large bonus payments for executives and very large stock plans. Incentive pay and stock constitute well over half the compensation of almost all executives today. Indeed, one could argue that many of the problems in the financial industry today are the result of pay plans motivating performance—the wrong kind of performance.

It is almost certain that the motivational power of executive compensation will be dramatically reduced by the pay provisions of any effort to control executive compensation. Not only does the TARP pay cap reduce the total amount of compensation available for incentive pay, it is likely that it will make it difficult to reward the correct behavior. As the many failures of executive compensation plans in the past have proven, it is difficult to get the right performance measures in place when it comes to executives and to be sure that they are paid adequately for the right behaviors. Government regulation is likely to make it more difficult. Indeed, if there are limitations on how much executives can make, it may lead to the unintentional elimination of incentive compensation for executives. Instead of focusing on designing incentive compensation plans, companies are likely to focus on finding ways to maximize executive pay under the regulations. Few companies are likely to put great amounts of executive compensation at risk when compensation is seen to be low because of government regulations.

One could argue that many of the problems in the financial industry today are the result of pay plans motivating performance—the wrong kind of performance.

In some cases, it may indeed be better to have no incentive pay rather than badly misguided plans that cause executives to do things that optimize only the short-term performance of an organization, or that are primarily targeted at being sure their bonus or stock plans pay off. The suggestion is often made that executive compensation should be limited primarily to bonuses and stock awards that are deferred in order to optimize the focus on longterm corporate performance. It is argued that combining this with the absence of large severance packages produces the right motivation package of incentive compensation. There is a lot of truth in this, but ultimately the issue is whether this is best accomplished through government regulation and whether it fits all organizations.

It is hard to imagine a series of government regulations and interventions that would create a situation in which most companies would end up with incentive compensation packages that fit their particular needs for performance. It is very much like the situation with respect to attracting and retaining the right executives. There are some general ground rules mat can be set, but it is hard for government to specify the right kinds of executive compensation plans, given the multitude of situations that companies find themselves in and the multitude of business strategies that they have.

Overall, it is hard to imagine regulations that would make incentive pay plans for executives more effective on a large scale. There is a chance that by specifying certain features mat are not allowable, like golden parachutes that reward failure, some malpractices can be eliminated, but that is about as far as it seems reasonable to take regulation with respect to incentive pay.

Impact on Corporate Culture and Reputation

The high level of executive compensation in the United States, especially when it is combined with poor organizational performance, has led to a negative image of the effectiveness of companies and has undermined the credibility of many executives. Particularly critical with respect to the amount of executive pay is the difference between the pay of top executives and the pay of lower level employees. This has been increasing for over two decades. In 2007, it was over 500-to-1 in large U.S. corporations, the highest in the developed world and in history. It is possible that by limiting the pay of senior executives, their pay level will become less of an issue with employees, investors and the general public. This, in turn, might make them be seen as more effective leaders and their organizations as being better managed.

There is little doubt that when a CEO's pay is more in line with that of other employees, it can increase their credibility as a leader and their credibility with investors. This has happened in companies where CEOs have restricted their total compensation to a level which is more in line with that of others in the organization and have been careful to create executive compensation packages that only reward them when the organization's performance warrants it. It gives them the ability to say they are in the same situation as the rest of the workforce and is often cited as an excellent leadership practice. Although leadership effectiveness is a subtle and hard-to-measure positive outcome of lower and better structured executive compensation plans, it is an important outcome.

Ironically, if regulations are implemented that force lower compensation levels on executives it may do more to subtract from the image of executives who voluntarily take lower and more appropriate compensation packages than it does to improve the image of others. There is a real danger that they will no longer get credit for having the right executive compensation pay level because in essence they will have to follow the government regulations like everybody else and no longer will be distinctive leaders who make good choices about their compensation.

Further, it is unclear that forcing executives to lower their compensation will give them any additional credibility or lead to their being more positively regarded by the workforce. It may have some effect because it will force them to "live more like the rest of the world," particularly if they do not have as much access to private jets and other extraordinary perquisites, but they will hardly get credit for the downsizing of their personal compensation if it is mandated by the government.

Overall, there may be more positive than negative effects from the government's limiting executive compensation when it comes to the public's regard for executives and, to some degree, for the regard they receive from their employees. A potential negative effect could be the loss of positive regard for those executives who voluntarily downsize their compensation packages. Of course, they can still do this by going beyond the regulations, and undoubtedly some will.

Perhaps the best overall conclusion with respect to the impact, both inside and outside of organizations, of regulations that reduce the total level of executive compensation is to say that they will be on balance positive but not particularly large or significant. Clearly, voluntary reductions on the part of executives would be much better.

The Right Approach

The scorecard with respect to the likely impact of government regulation of executive compensation is not favorable. This raises the question of whether there is a better alternative, and I think there is. Executive compensation is the responsibility of corporate boards; they need to do a better job, but are unlikely to unless governance changes are made. My research shows that 31% of board members feel CEO pay is too high in most cases; another 47% feel it is too high in a few high-profile cases. These feelings are unlikely to lead to action, however, since 85% feel their companies' CEO pay program is effective. However, there are two key governance changes that might lead to boards creating more effective executive compensation plans.

The first is to require that all boards separate the role of CEO and board chair. This is common in Europe and it may not be accidental that compensation levels are much lower in Europe. In Europe, however, the chair is often a former CEO of the company and cannot be described as an independent chair. In order to have an effective chair, the chair needs to be independent of the company and its executives. This is more likely to lead to a board that makes tough decisions about how executives are paid.

The second change is putting executive compensation plans to a vote of the shareholders, for whom the CEO and top executives ultimately work. Because shareholders are "the boss," they are the logical ones to determine CEO compensation. A first step, which has been taken by less than a dozen major companies, is to make the vote advisory. If this doesn't constrain CEO compensation, then it is important to move on to a mandatory shareholder vote on all top executive compensation plans.

There are a number of pros and cons associated with shareholder votes, but it is the change most likely to leave companies with the opportunity to design effective compensation plans without government intervention—and at the same time satisfy shareholders with respect to the level of CEO compensation. If it fails to have its intended effect then, and only then, should we consider government-mandated restrictions on executive compensation payments.

One final thought: There is a chance that by moving now to reduce executive compensation levels and improve corporate governance, CEOs and boards can prevent further government regulation of executive compensation.

Organizations to Contact

The editors have compiled the following list of organizations concerned with the issues debated in this book. The descriptions are derived from materials provided by the organizations. All have publications or information available for interested readers. The list was compiled on the date of publication of the present volume; the information provided here may change. Be aware that many organizations take several weeks or longer to respond to inquiries, so allow as much time as possible.

American Bankers Association (ABA)

1120 Connecticut Avenue, NW, Washington, DC   20036
(800) 226-5377
website: http://www.aba.com

The ABA was established in 1875 and represents banks of all sizes and charters. The issues it focuses on include corporate governance and disclosure, mortgage lending, and pro-business tax policies. The ABA publishes the *Reference Guide for Regulatory Compliance* and the *ABA Bank Compliance*.

The American Federation of Labor and Congress of Industrial Organizations (AFL-CIO)

815 16th Street, NW, Washington, DC   20006
(202) 637-5018
website: http://afcio.org

The AFL-CIO was established in 1955 when the AFL merged with the CIO. A voluntary federation of 55 national and international labor unions, the AFL-CIO works to improve the lives of working families by bringing economic justice to the workplace and social justice to the nation. One of the advocacy tools that the AFL-CIO uses to keep people informed about corporate injustices is Corporate Watch. *Facts & Stats*, speeches, and testimony are available on the website.

Cato Institute

1000 Massachusetts Avenue, NW
Washington, DC   20001-5403
(202) 842-0200 • fax: (202) 842-3490
website: www.cato.org

Founded in 1997, the Cato Institute is a public-policy research think tank that promotes individual liberty, limited government, free markets, and peace. The Cato Institute is opposed to excessive government power. Its publications include *Policy Analysis, Regulation,* and the *Tax & Budget Bulletin.*

Center for Corporate Policy

P.O. Box 19405, Washington, DC   20036
(202) 387-8030 • fax:(202) 234-5176
email: info@corporatepolicy.org
website: www.corporatepolicy.org

The mission of the Center for Corporate Policy is to rein in corporate abuses and hold companies publicly responsible for their actions. The Center's issues include executive compensation, corporate crime and abuse, and corporations and the Constitution. Online publications include fact sheets about corporate responsibility.

Center on Executive Compensation

1100 13th Street, NW, Suite 850, Washington, DC   20005
(202) 408-8181 • fax: (202) 789-0064
email: info@execcomp.org
website: www.execcomp.org

The Center on Executive Compensation was established by the board of directors of the HR Policy Association, a nonprofit public policy organization representing the chief human resource officers of hundreds of corporations. Its goal is to advance and develop salary and governance practices and advocate for compensation packages that reflect the best interests of shareholders and other corporate stakeholders. Publications include *Say on Pay Versus Mandatory Votes on Pay* and *Executive Compensation from the Perspective of the Largest Institutional Investors.*

Financial Services Roundtable

1001 Pennsylvania Avenue, NW, Washington, DC 20004
(202) 289-4322 • fax: (202) 628-2507
email: info@fsround.org
website: http://fsround.org

The mission of the Financial Services Roundtable is to promote and protect the economic vitality and integrity of the US financial system and of its members. It achieves its mission by legislative and regulatory advocacy, a trusted reputation in the industry, and executive leadership forums. The Roundtable's publications include *Systemic Risk Implementation: Recommendations to the Financial Stability Oversight Council and the Office of Financial Research* and *Assessing the Impact of Proposed Federal Reserve Debit Interchange Policy.*

Institute for America's Future

1825 K Street, NW, Suite 400, Washington, DC 20006
(202) 955-5665 • fax: (202) 955-5606
website: http://institute.ourfuture.org

The mission of the Institute for America's Future is to build support for progressive government and challenge conservative policies through research and education. The Institute focuses on such issues as the need to curb Wall Street, to increase quality education, and to provide health care for all. Its publications include *Big Bank Takeover: How-Too-Big-To-Fail's Army of Lobbyists Has Captured Washington* and the fact sheet *Essentials for Financial Reform.*

Institute for Policy Studies (IPS)

1112 16th Street, NW, Suite 600, Washington, DC 20036
(202) 234-9382
email: info@ips-dc.org
website: www.ips-dc.org

The mission of the IPS is to encourage true democracy and confront corporate influence, concentrated wealth, and military power. The IPS works with social movements to connect peace, justice, and the environment in the United States and around the world. Its reports include *Executive Excess 2010: CEO Pay and the Great Recession* and *Executive Pay and the Stimulus Bill.*

Public Company Accounting Oversight Board (PCAOB)

1666 K Street, NW, Washington, DC   20006-2803
(202) 207-9100 • fax: (202) 862-8430
website: http://pcaob.org

Established by Congress as part of the Sarbanes-Oxley Act of 2002, the PCAOB is a nonprofit corporation that protects investors by overseeing the audits of public companies, as well as preparing independent audit reports. The Sarbanes-Oxley Act states that the auditors of public companies in the United States can no longer be self-regulating; such auditors are now subject to independent and external oversight. The PCAOB's publications include *Staff Alert Practice Audits* and research reports.

US Securities and Exchange Commission (SEC)

100 F Street, NE, Washington, DC   20549
(202) 942-8088
website: http://sec.gov

The SEC's purpose is to ensure that markets are efficient, orderly, and fair; make capital formation possible; and protect investors. It also is responsible for the Dodd-Frank Wall Street Reform and Consumer Protection Act, which was signed into law in 2010 and is intended, among other things, to protect investors and consumers and to regulate executive compensation. Publications include the *SEC News Digest* and *SEC Special Studies*, which are available online.

Bibliography

Books

Viral V. Acharya, et al.	*Regulating Wall Street: The Dodd-Frank Act and the New Architecture of Global Finance.* Hoboken, N.J.: John Wiley & Sons, 2010.
Viral V. Acharya, et al.	*Guaranteed to Fail: Fannie Mae, Freddie Mac, and the Debacle of Mortgage Finance.* Princeton, N.J.: Princeton University Press, 2011.
Lucian Bebchuk and Jess Fried	*Pay Without Performance: The Unfulfilled Promise of Executive Compensation.* Boston, Mass.: Harvard University Press, 2004.
Roddy Boyd	*Fatal Risk: A Cautionary Tale of AIG's Corporate Suicide.* Hoboken, N.J.: John Wiley & Sons, 2011.
William Cohan	*House of Cards: A Tale of Hubris and Wretched Excess on Wall Street.* New York: Doubleday, 2009.
Committee on Oversight and Government Reform, US House of Representatives	*Executive Compensation: How Much Is Too Much?* Washington, D.C.: US Government Printing Office, 2010.
Bruce Ellig	*The Complete Guide to Executive Compensation.* New York: McGraw-Hill, 2007.

Ira T. Kay and Steve van Putten	*Myths and Realities of Executive Pay.* New York: Cambridge University Press, 2007.
Walter Kiechel	*The Lords of Strategy: The Secret Intellectual History of the New Corporate World.* Boston, Mass.: Harvard Business School Press, 2010.
Robert W. Kolb	*The Ethics of Executive Compensation.* Hoboken, N.J.: Wiley-Blackwell, 2006.
Les Leopold	*The Looting of America: How Wall Street's Game of Fantasy Finance Destroyed Our Jobs, Pensions and Prosperity and What We Can Do About It.* White River Junction, Vt.: Chelsea Green Publishing, 2009.
Michael Lewis	*The Big Short: Inside the Doomsday Machine.* New York: W.W. Norton & Company, 2010.
Roger Lowenstein	*The End of Wall Street.* New York: Penguin Press, 2011.
Jonathan R. Macey	*Corporate Governance: Promises Kept, Promises Broken.* Princeton, N.J.: Princeton University Press, 2010.
Bethany McLean and Joe Nocera	*All the Devils Are Here: The Hidden History of the Financial Crisis.* New York: Portfolio Hardcover, 2010.
Mercer	*Pay for Results: Aligning Executive Compensation With Business Performance.* Hoboken, N.J.: John Wiley & Sons, 2009.

Gretchen Morgenson — *Reckless Endangerment: How Outsized Ambition, Greed, and Corruption Led to Economic Armageddon.* New York: Times Books, 2011.

Johan Norberg — *Financial Fiasco: How America's Infatuation with Home Ownership and Easy Money Created the Economic Crisis.* Washington, D.C.: Cato Institute, 2009.

Raghuram G. Rajan — *Fault Lines: How Hidden Fractures Still Threaten the World Economy.* Princeton, N.J.: Princeton University Press, 2010.

Mariana S. Ramirez, ed. — *"Say on Pay" and Executive Compensation Issues.* Hauppauge, N.Y.: Nova Publishers, 2011.

David Skeel and William D. Cohan — *The New Financial Deal: Understanding the Dodd-Frank Act and Its (Unintended) Consequences.* Hoboken, N.J.: John Wiley & Sons, 2010.

Andres Ross Sorkin — *Too Big to Fail: The Inside Story of How Wall Street and Washington Fought to Save the Financial System—and Themselves.* New York: Penguin, 2009.

Gregory P. Wilson — *Managing to the New Regulatory Reality: Doing Business Under the Dodd-Frank Act.* Hoboken, N.J.: John Wiley & Sons, 2011.

Periodicals and Internet Sources

John J. Brennan "Improving Corporate Governance: A Memo to the Board," *The Wall Street Journal*, May 10, 2010.

Mark S. Calabria "Regulating Executive Pay," *The Economist*, August 16, 2010.

Dawn Cowie "Remuneration: Banks Fine-Tune Their Bonus Systems," *Euromoney*, August 2010.

Steven M. Davidoff "In Regulator's Proposal, Incentive for Excessive Risk Remains," *The New York Times*, April 13, 2011.

Bruce R. Ellig "Excessive Executive Pay Can Be Stopped," *Workspan*, November 2006.

Ray Fisman "Comparison Shopping: The Real Reason CEO Compensation Got Out of Hand," www.slate.com, May 11, 2009.

David R. Francis "How Long Will Politicians Look the Other Way on CEO Pay?" *The Christian Science Monitor*, August 25, 2008.

David R. Francis "Are CEOs Worth 300 More Times Than Their Lowest-Paid Workers?" *The Christian Science Monitor*, March 15, 2011.

Rob Garver "Exempt from, But Influenced by, Dodd-Frank Restrictions," *American Banker*, March 22, 2011.

Kathy Kristof   "Blame High Executive Pay on
                       Corporate Boards,"
                       www.townhall.com, June 15, 2009.

David Lazarus   "It's Time for Boards to Crack Down
                       on CEO Pay," *Los Angeles Times*, May
                       24, 2009.

Eugene A. Ludwig   "Times Have Changed: CEOs Must
and Neil Smith   Do the Same," *American Banker*,
                       October 16, 2009.

Jonathan Macey   "'Say on Pay' and Other Bad Ideas,"
                       Wall Street Journal, April 14, 2009.

Kathleen Pender   "How Corporations Avoid Paying
                       Federal Taxes," *San Francisco
                       Chronicle*, April 21, 2011.

Edmund S.   "The Economy Needs a Bit of
Phelps   Ingenuity," *The New York Times*,
                       August 7, 2010.

Richard D. Quinn   "Quinn Applies Newton's Third Law
                       to Benefits," *Employee Benefit News*,
                       June 15, 2006.

Ann Rhoades   "Easing the Transition to the New
                       Rules on Compensation,"
                       Directorship, February/March 2011.

John Paul Rollert   "Goldman Sachs Bonuses: More
                       Than Just Bad PR," *The Christian
                       Science Monitor*, December 18, 2009.

Judith F.   "Are Executives Paid Too Much?" *The
Samuelson and   Wall Street Journal*, February 26,
Lynn A. Stout   2009.

George Skelton — "Message to UC Execs: If It Won't Look Good in the Newspaper, Don't Do It," *Los Angeles Times*, February 16, 2006.

Ginger Szala — "More of the Same?" *Futures*, January 2011.

Laura Vanderkam — "Cracking the CEO Pay Puzzle," *The American*, March/April. 2008.

Jack Welch and Suzy Welch — "CEO Pay: NO Easy Answer," *Business Week*, July 14, 2008.

Greg Wilson — "Making Dodd-Frank Work," *American Banker*, February 16, 2011.

Index

A

Advisers, compensation committee, 34
Anderson, Sarah, 59
Athletes, 16, 43, 65
Attracting and retaining executives, 67, 85–87
Automobile industry, 51–52

B

Bailouts, 51–52, 64–65, 74–75
Basulto, Dominic, 15
Boards of directors, 68–73, 91
Buffett, Warren, 76–77
Business self-regulation, 10, 14, 91–92

C

Calbreath, Dean, 48
Calculations, executive-worker pay ratios, 27–28, 37–38
Calhoun, David, 20
Capitalism. *See* Free market system
Chief executive officers
  business self-regulation, 91–92
  compensation restraints, 23
  executive-worker pay ratio trends, 76
  hiring and firing practices, 16–20
  median pay, 32–33
  performance goals, 20–22
  salary trends, 52–53

"say on pay" legislative provision, 24–29
tax subsidized salaries, 62–63
underperforming companies, 31–32
Collateralized debt obligations, 76–80
Compensation committees
  conflicts of interest, 34
  fair compensation principles, 71–72
  performance formulas, 33–34
  policy establishment, 10, 14
  underperforming companies, 32
Competition, 45–47, 55–56
Conflicts of interest, 34
Corporate culture, 89–90
Corporate growth and resources, 71
The Corporate Library, 32
Corporate raiders, 44–45, 46
Cost control measures, corporate, 30–31
Crawford, Stephen, 37
Credibility issues, 89–90
Crook, Clive, 30

D

Deregulation, 75–76
Disclosure, 24–29, 33–35, 67
Dodd-Frank legislation proposal, 24–29
Drucker, Peter, 62